WISDOM
PROMISE
GIVE
RESULT

WISDOM
LEARN FAST
MVB
NO BULLSH*T

NO BULLSH*T BRANDING

A Step-by-Step Guide to Discover, Design, and Deliver Your Brand

JAMES MARTIN

ROCKPORT

Quarto.com

First published in 2026 by Rockport Publishers, an imprint of The Quarto Group,
100 Cummings Center, Suite 265-D, Beverly, MA 01915, USA.
T (978) 282-9590 F (978) 283-2742

EEA Representation, WTS Tax d.o.o.,
Žanova ulica 3, 4000 Kranj, Slovenia.
www.wts-tax.si

Rockport Publishers titles are also available at discount for retail, wholesale, promotional, and bulk purchase. For details, contact the Special Sales Manager by email at specialsales@quarto.com or by mail at The Quarto Group, Attn: Special Sales Manager, 100 Cummings Center, Suite 265-D, Beverly, MA 01915, USA.

10 9 8 7 6 5 4 3 2 1

ISBN: 978-1-57715-945-2

Digital edition published in 2026
eISBN: 978-1-57715-946-9

Library of Congress Control Number: 2026939234

Design: James Martin, Kiel Tillman, Paul Balfe
Cover Image: James Martin, Kiel Tillman, Paul Balfe
Page Layout: Paul Balfe
Illustration: Kiel Tillman, James Martin, Lincoln Design Co.

Printed in Guangdong, China TT062026

For the designers bold enough to lead.

You are not your job title.
You are not a cog in the system.
You are not here to live out someone else's version of success.

You are a role the world needs. A creative partner, a builder, a liberator of ideas. A thinker. A guide. A collaborator.

You get to choose what you stand for, and how you show up.

May this book help you step fully into that role,turn clarity into power,and bring something real into the world on your own terms.

No fluff. No gatekeepers. No bullsh*t.

Your ideas matter.
The world is waiting.

Build The Real Brand Life:
A life where your creativity, character, and career align.

MBJ Made BY JAMES

CONTENTS:

Section Four —
BUILDING YOUR MVB

Section Five —
LAUNCH WITHOUT PANIC

"CREATIVITY IS THE PROCESS OF HAVING ORIGINAL IDEAS THAT HAVE VALUE."

– Sir Ken Robinson

REAL TALK

When I was at school, being "the creative one" wasn't exactly a badge of honour. It was more of a shrug, a sideways glance, sometimes even the punchline to a teacher's joke in front of the class.

"Ah, James, he's the arty one."
"He's not the academic type."
"He'll struggle in the real world."

If you're reading this, there's a good chance you've had those same labels. Maybe you were the one doodling in the margins while the science teacher rolled their eyes. Maybe you dressed a little too wacky and were told no "real" job would ever allow it. Maybe you were branded the unorganised, disruptive one simply because you never did things "the right way."

Yup . . . me too.

The truth is, creative people are really fuc*ing messy. We don't fit neatly in boxes, we don't always follow the rules, and we rarely produce the kind of answers you can tick off with a red pen at exam time. And because of that, for decades (maybe even centuries), we've been pushed to the sidelines.

But here comes the first of many plot twists. The very things the world dismissed for so long, the oddness, the mess, the crazy imagination, are actually the things that make you incredibly valuable. People remind us daily to be wary of AI and automation, but the machines can only dream of connecting dots the way we do. I'm not dismissing how disruptive the technology is right now, but our weirdness, our unpredictability, our chaos: That is our superpower.

The problem was that back at school, most of us were never taught to see it that way. While we were busy collecting labels, laughing off the jokes, or brushing off the sideways glances, something bigger was happening. Those reputations were shaping our identity. When I was called "the arty one," it wasn't just a throwaway comment. It was a reputation that painted me as "less than," and I carried it far beyond the classroom. I think this is why so many creative people wrestle with crippling self-doubt. They don't always see their own value, because for most of their lives they were branded by school and society as "not important." Those early reputations stick, and they continue to shape how we see ourselves today.

Whether you've thought about it or not, you already are a living, breathing brand. The films you rave about, the way you order your frothy coffee, the trainers you wear, the playlists you share, even how you apologise when you show up late—all of those choices, habits, and signals add up to a reputation.

But reputation doesn't just live in your head. It lives in the way other people experience you and the stories they tell about you. It shows up in the way your family talks about you, in how your friends describe you, in what your colleagues expect from you at work. People already have a sense of who you are and what you stand for, whether you've ever thought about it or not.

Take my son, Rocco, as an example. He's only two, but he already has a reputation in our family. He's the wild, energetic spirit who is kind and confident around everyone he meets. There's evidence to back this up. He eats food off the floor, spends most of his time without any clothes on, belts out "Hakuna Matata" at full shout volume even though he doesn't know the words, and he gives his new toys to friends who come over to play. All of that evidence builds his reputation, which shapes his identity, and in turn forms the way people see him: his brand. And he's never once tried to build it.

And that's really what I want you to take from this introduction: the importance of reputation. **My great friend Kevin Finn says it best when he calls a brand "a recognisable reputation."** Branding is simply the habit of shaping the reputation you already have into something clear, consistent, and recognisable. And the way you do that is with evidence, the proof in how you show up, what you deliver, and how people experience you. But evidence alone doesn't build trust. Later in the book, we'll look at how perception plays its part, but let's save that juicy treat for later.

When most people hear the word "branding," they picture expensive workshops, giant decks, and super glossy campaigns. Useful later, sure. But that's not the heart of it. The heart of branding has always been human. At its simplest, a brand says, "This is us. This is what you can expect. You can trust this." In this book, we're going to keep it human, keep it useful, and make sure we're building brands properly from the ground up.

Now, here's why this matters for you as a designer. Every piece of work you do, every poster, logo, type choice, colour palette, or presentation, is helping your client build their reputation. It's not just decoration; it's an accumulation of evidence. When you start looking at branding this way, it makes your role easier to explain, easier to justify, and easier to value. Your role becomes clear. You help your clients earn and express a reputation people can trust.

But let's flip it for a second. This isn't only about your clients; it's about you, too.

Most designers pour their best energy into other people's ideas and leave their own gathering dust. We'll spend hours pushing pixels for our clients, but can't bring ourselves to share our own work. We'll fight for someone else's idea, but leave our own scribbles in a drawer. We all do this. But here's the thing: You are already sitting on mountains of evidence. The projects you've delivered, the style you've refined, the ideas filling your notebooks. That's your reputation waiting to be shaped. And if you start treating yourself as the builder, not just the executor, you can begin shaping not only your own ideas but also the future you want to step into.

This book is an invitation to explore two powerful paths that can change the way you work and create.

The Creative Partner Path helps you step up from executor to collaborator. You'll learn how to guide clarity, shape direction, and build trust with clients, not just through the work you make, but through the way you frame and lead it.

The Idea Liberator Path gives you the tools and confidence to finally back yourself. To take the messy, brilliant ideas you've been sitting on and turn them into something real. To own your identity, shift your reputation, and stop waiting for permission.

That's the unlock. This is a client-facing tool kit and a personal reputation-builder rolled into one delicious snack.

So, if you've picked up this book, it's probably for one of two reasons. Either the sweary cover caught your eye, or you want to get a clearer handle on branding, not just for your clients, but for yourself, too. Whatever brought you here, you're in the right place.

You'll find stories from my own journey, lessons I've learned from other brilliant people, little bits of science that explain how our brains actually tick, and practical frameworks that will help you turn raw ideas into real brands. For years, I was the guy who purely executed for clients and I left my own ideas in the wings, waiting for the "perfect" moment to build them. Eventually, I realised there is no perfect moment, just the choice to begin. That choice changed everything for me.

I started carving out time for my own ideas. At first, it was small things like sharing my process online, posting messy sketches, letting people peek behind the curtain of my process. But those little steps snowballed into much bigger things, like my first book, courses, my own design studio, creative communities, merch, brand workshops, even SaaS products. None of it began perfectly. It was raw, fuzzy, and imperfect, but I put the ideas out anyway.

And here's the wild part. Those messy ideas opened doors I never could have planned for. They led me to become a creative partner at my dream design studio, Lincoln Design Co. They got me a seat on the design advisory board at Canva. They even put me in an advisory role at Affinity, helping shape pro design tools used by creatives all over the world.

Lincoln Design Co Team & sketches

Those ideas, those experiments, weren't just opportunities. They gave me the ability to reshape my own reputation. They gave me an identity. A brand. For years I carried the label of "the arty one," but by putting my own ideas into the world, I built a new story. I wasn't just the messy creative anymore, I became the human people turned to for advice, for design, for ideas, for partnerships, for friendships. That's the beautiful thing about reputation: it's not fixed. You can change it. You can own it.

And that, my friends, is liberating.

I want to be clear. This book is about starting. About giving you and your clients the tools to move when most people end up stalling. It's not about deep-dive archetypes, twelve-week strategy sessions, or omni-channel brand theatre. That stuff has its place, apparently, but let's be honest, most of our clients don't have the budget, patience, or need for it when they're just starting out. And neither do you when it comes to your own ideas. What you need is something leaner. Something that builds clarity fast, creates momentum, and lets you test and learn without burning through time or cash.

That's where the Minimum Viable Brand (MVB) comes in.

The MVB is both a mindset shift and a practical tool designed to help you and your clients build the smallest useful version of a brand so ideas can move, earn, and grow. I first used it for myself, because I was tired of leaving my own ideas to waste in a drawer. Then, I realised it was just as powerful for my clients, especially for those who didn't have a big budget but still needed support to move their ideas ahead. It's simple, scrappy, and built for anyone ready to give their idea a real shot. For your clients, it's a sharp way to test and learn before committing big money. For you, it's a way to finally back yourself and start building the ideas you've been sitting on.

I'm not here to claim ownership of the MVB concept. Variations of this approach have been floating around for years, and plenty of designers have probably used it in practice without giving it a name. My hope is simply that more designers use it going forward, because it's useful, helpful, and it will help you grow your business.

The idea originated from Eric Ries's *The Lean Startup*. He introduced the Minimum Viable Product (MVP), the smallest useful version of a product that lets you learn, adapt, and grow. It's a mindset shift that saves you from the paralysis of "perfect later" and gets you moving now.

To build the MVB, we'll use my framework, the Five Idea Keys. It's a no-bullsh*t system I've honed over the last decade working closely with clients. I originally built it to give me structure on discovery calls so I could quickly get to the truth, ask better questions, and get to clarity faster. For years, it was just how I worked, but in the last couple of years, I finally gave it a name.

Together, the MVB and the Five Idea Keys give you something most designers don't have: a way to guide the messy early stage. For your clients, it means sharper conversations, stronger briefs, and decisions that make sense. For you, it means a repeatable way to back your own ideas, test them, and finally see what they can become.

And here's the bigger shift. Once you start using these tools, you'll stop seeing yourself as just the pixel pusher. You'll step into the role of Creative Partner and Idea Liberator, roles that aren't just useful for you, but essential in the new creative age we're entering.

That's the power in this new world. Not more jargon. Not more waiting, but more action. More ideas moving. More reputations built. And more designers like you stepping up to shape culture, not just serve it.

By the time you finish this book, you won't just understand branding. You'll see yourself differently, as someone shaping ideas, building reputations, and owning your identity with confidence.

So, are you ready to rock and roll?

LFG.

NEVER BURNS OUT!
THE MBJ HOTEL
MBJ Made BY JAMES
DESIGNER EDUCATOR AUTHOR
FATHER HUSBAND
I AM A 'HIGH SCHOOL' KICKED OUT
I AM AN OFFICIAL D.A.B-BER
I RUN A 'SUPER DUPER' STUDIO
CREATIVE PARTNER AT LDC

THE NO BULLSH*T PLEDGE

I am a creative thinker.
I am not here to play small.
I am not here to wait for permission.
I am here to build.

I will claim my creativity as a superpower.
I will use it to shape ideas into reality.
I will not dismiss my vision as “just an idea.”
I will stand behind it and make it real.

I will choose clarity over chaos.
I will choose action over hesitation.
I will choose progress over perfection.

No fluff.
No fear.
No bullsh*t.

The future belongs to people who think creatively.
That means the future belongs to me.

Signed: ______________________________

Foreword by Lisa Smith

NO BULLSH*T, NO BARRIERS

The title of this book sums up its author perfectly: no bullsh*t, no fluff, no over-academic spiel. Just straight to the point, real, and full of honesty.

I first met James when we were both invited to join the design advisory board at Canva. That board's packed with some of the most talented, thoughtful, and, let's be honest, intimidatingly brilliant people you'll ever meet. That curation didn't happen by accident. Thank you, Monica, Cat, and Andrew, for putting together a lineup of minds and misfits who see the world differently.

When I met James in Sydney, I knew right away this guy wasn't your typical "design thought leader." What's a "design thought leader," anyway? Exactly. Whatever that is, he wasn't it. He didn't try to impress anyone. He wasn't dropping buzzwords or flexing credentials. He was just himself: sharp as hell, grounded, funny, and completely uninterested in playing the "design guru" game.

It wasn't long before we were deep in conversation about accessibility and how design should belong to everyone. And believe me, we've both had to defend that view more times than we can count. The elite design crowd often feels threatened by the very existence of Canva, too short-sighted to see that the real value isn't in the tools but in what people make with them.

With that shared perspective, we hit it off straight away. On the outside, we couldn't have been more different—one of us from Hampshire, the other from Essex—but underneath, we were cut from the same cloth. We've both had our own versions of rock bottom, and we've both clawed our way back through hard work, stubborn optimism, and the belief that what we do can actually make a difference. A combination of grit, realism, and hope.

What I love about James is that everything he does, he does with intention. There's no performance, no pretending, no ego trip. He doesn't hide behind fancy words, and believe me, I've seen some fancy words. Some of the most elite schools and agencies churn out people with vocabularies built to sound clever but who say absolutely nothing. Clients do it too, making their problems sound like rocket science until you ask them to explain it like you're five.

Thank God for people like James who just say it like it is, with clarity, compassion, and a bit of humour that makes even the uncomfortable stuff go down easier. That's exactly what this book is. ***No Bullsh*t Branding*** is James on paper: straight-talking, smart, grounded, and deeply human.

Before you dive in, let me tell you what this book isn't. It's not another shiny marketing book full of jargon and diagrams. It's not about finding your "synergy" or crafting your "authentic voice" through some twelve-step model. It's about cutting through the noise and getting to what really matters—who you are, what you stand for, and how you show up every single day.

And here's the best part: It doesn't have to be perfect.

Because let's be honest, most of what passes for branding advice is absolute nonsense. Everyone's preaching "purpose" and "storytelling," but few can explain it without disappearing into buzzword soup. James slices straight through that mess and reminds us that branding isn't what you say, it's what you do. It's how people feel after they've interacted with you.

That's the genius of his approach. It's not about perfection, it's about consistency. It's about showing up as your true self, not the version you think the world wants.

I've watched James in rooms full of big names, and he's never changed his tone or softened his truth. He'll call out the fluff, ask the hard questions, and make people actually think. And somehow, he does it with kindness. That balance of tough love and empathy is rare.

He's also one of the most generous people I know. He shares his lessons, his scars, his philosophies—not to show off, but to lift others up. He believes in community over competition, and that's exactly the kind of energy this book radiates.

Reading ***No Bullsh*t Branding*** feels less like reading a business book and more like sitting down with a mate who's been there, done it, and is willing to tell you the truth you probably need to hear, even if it stings a bit. He'll challenge you to rethink what branding actually means. He'll push you to stop hiding behind logos and taglines and start focusing on the experience you create. He'll show you that honesty isn't just moral, it's magnetic.

Because the world doesn't need more polished brands. It needs more genuine ones. Brands built on trust, not tricks. Brands that make promises and actually keep them.

That's what James stands for. That's what this book stands for.

So get comfortable; you're not about to read another self-congratulatory business book. You're about to learn how to strip it all back and build something real.

Something with heart.
Something with grit.
Something with zero bullsh*t.

That's James. That's this book. And that's exactly why it matters.

Lisa Smith is a globally respected creative leader with over two decades of experience shaping some of the world's most iconic brands. As global chief design officer at Uncommon Studios, she drives the agency's mission to make design central to everything it creates—building brands that capture attention and shape culture.

Previously, she served as global executive creative director at JKR, helping transform it from a packaging agency into a full-spectrum branding powerhouse through landmark rebrands for Walmart, Burger King, Mozilla, Uber, and more. Her earlier roles include ECD at Chobani—where she led a creative transformation that fuelled growth—and head of design at Wolff Olins New York, delivering bold work for The Met, USA Today, and Zocdoc.

Named one of Fast Company's Most Creative People, Lisa has had work featured in *The New York Times*, *Forbes*, and *Fast Company*, and has earned top industry honours, including a Cannes Gold Lion, multiple Fast Company awards, and leadership roles as jury president at Cannes Lions and D&AD.

Lisa Smith
Global chief design officer at Uncommon Creative Studio and president of the D&AD

SECTION ONE

HOW BRANDING LOST ITS WAY

Alright, before we dive into all the juicy bits . . . the studio chats, the case studies, the Minimum Viable Brand (MVB) magic, I want us to take a little step back.

If we're going to move forward with confidence, it helps to understand how we got here in the first place. Because somewhere along the way, branding started to lose its way. The conversation got louder, the jargon got thicker, and before long, what used to be about creativity and connection turned into confusion and chaos.

Now, this isn't a blame game. It's not your fault, and it's not really the industry's fault either. It's just what happens when something good gets overcooked. Branding became big business. Everyone wanted a piece of it. And in the process, we all kind of forgot what it was actually for: helping ideas make sense to people.

So, this first section is about clearing the ground. Think of it like tidying your desk before a big project. We're going to dig into a few of the myths, the mindsets, and the branding fluff that's been tripping us creative humans up for years.

Once you can see how branding got tangled, you can start to untangle it. And when you do that, everything gets easier . . . the work, the conversations, the confidence. You start building brands the way they were meant to be built: with intention, with care, and with a bit of creative mischief along the way.

So . . . let's crack on.

ESTD
ARTIST
FOR CREATIVES
BY CREATIVES

Chapter One -

A QUICK HISTORY OF BRANDING

A quick note before we start, friends. I'm not a historian or a psychologist. No surprises there. This is my take on how branding evolved over the years. Think of it as a designer's cheat sheet rather than a lecture.

A quick rewind that skips the trivia and focuses on how branding drifted from something deeply human into something far more complicated, and why that matters for the work you do today.

Before brands were logos or shop signs, they were about something far more human: belonging. People have always needed some sort of connection to a family, a tribe, a community. Psychologists call it the "need to belong." It sits alongside food and sleep as a basic human requirement.

We showed that belonging through visible markers like war paint, clan tartans, feathers, jewellery, and tattoos. These weren't brands in the modern sense, but they worked the same way. They made identity visible. At a glance, you knew who was with you, who wasn't, and whether the person running toward you with a sword was someone to hug or someone to run away from.

A tartan wasn't just fabric. It was identity.
A tattoo wasn't just decoration. It told a story.
A feather wasn't just an accessory. It signalled rank and deeds.

Different things, same purpose: to show who you were.

Of course, it didn't stay that way. Over time, the layers built up, cultures shifted, and new industries appeared. And when that happens, things inevitably get complicated, especially once money enters the picture. But before we dive into the mess, let's start at the beginning.

Stage One: BRANDING AS FUNCTION

At the very beginning, branding was as simple as it gets. It was purely functional.

Farmers heated up an iron and marked their cattle so they could tell one herd from another. Craftsmen carved or stamped their initials into tools, pots, or furniture so buyers knew who made them. Shopkeepers painted "Bakery" or "Blacksmith" on a wooden sign so people passing by could see what they sold.

Branding began as pure function, a marker of ownership. No story, no emotion, no trend.

Key Takeaway: Branding started as a tag. Nothing more.

Stage Two: THE INDUSTRIAL BOOM

The 1800s shook things up. The Industrial Revolution meant goods weren't just made by the bloke down the street anymore. Flour, soap, and fabric were now mass produced. Instead of buying bread from John the Baker who knew your name, you were buying from a company miles away.

Which created a new problem: How do I know I can actually trust this stuff?

The answer was consistent details, packaging, and trademarks. That flour in the blue sack? Yes, that's the one I bought last time, I'll grab it again. We humans love shortcuts, and a familiar signal helps us decide more quickly and feel safe.

Branding tapped into something deeply human: our love of consistency. We trust what we recognise. If something delivers on its promise again and again, we keep going back. Which, let's be honest, is probably why you always end up at the same restaurant or grab the same stuff from the fridge without even thinking about it.

Key Takeaway: Branding turned into a trust signal.

Stage Three: THE ASPIRATIONAL MAD MEN

Alright, I'm skipping ahead a bit, but let's land in the mid-twentieth century. Advertising explodes, television shows up in most homes, and suddenly brands aren't just fighting for space on the shelf, they're fighting for space in your head.

Welcome to Madison Avenue. Sharp suits, smoke-filled offices, and a shiny new realisation: If you can shape perception, you can shape desire.

Agencies stopped just flogging products and started building entire worlds around them. Coca-Cola wasn't just fizzy water; it was happiness in a bottle. Marlboro wasn't just cigarettes; it was rugged masculinity in a red-and-white box. Volkswagen wasn't just a car; it was rebellion on four wheels.

By now, it wasn't enough for something to work; it had to mean something. We used brands to say, "This is who I am," or sometimes, "This is who I'd like you to think I am."

This was when branding turned into full-blown theatre. The product became the stage, the customer the actor, and the brand the script that tricked you into playing along. And yes, as a kid desperate to look cool, those Marlboros definitely did a number on me. (Don't smoke, kids.)

Madison Avenue didn't invent belonging; they just bottled it, scaled it, and sold it back with a jingle.

Key Takeaway: Branding turned into theatre.

Stage Four:
THE CORPORATE EXPLOSION

By the late twentieth century, branding had gone big. Really big.

Corporations weren't just selling one product anymore. They were juggling entire families of brands across countries and categories. And the bigger they grew, the messier it got.

Suddenly, there were brand manuals thick enough to prop up a house and focus groups nobody read. Whole teams existed just to keep things "on brand."

At that scale, it made sense. If you've got thousands of employees and products across the globe, you need systems to stop chaos. But to everyone outside those boardrooms, branding started to look like a closed club. Something only mega-corporations with mega-budgets could touch. For the everyday human, it suddenly felt out of reach.

Key Takeaway: Branding ballooned into complexity.

Stage Five:
THE DOT-COM BOOM

Then along came the internet. Businesses were popping up faster than you could count them. The 1990s were full of wild ideas and money spraying around like a busted fire hose. Startups with no revenue and zero customers were raising millions, sometimes just on the strength of a pitch deck and a dream.

To convince investors you were the next big thing, you had to look like it.

This wasn't about trickery; it was reassurance. Humans love shortcuts, especially when judging risk. In the dot-com era, branding became that shortcut. If your company looked the part, investors felt safer betting on you.

Key Takeaway: Branding became a shortcut to legitimacy.

Stage Six:
THE SOCIAL MEDIA TREADMILL

By the 2010s, social media flipped branding on its head, and we're all still sweating from the workout.

Before social, most brands refreshed occasionally. A new logo every couple of decades, a big campaign every few years. Nice and steady. Then Facebook, Instagram, and Twitter (now X) showed up and blew that rhythm apart. Suddenly, it wasn't about the occasional refresh, it was about a constant stream. Every post, story, tweet, or video had to say something.

Branding stopped being patient work and became performance. Every single day.

The content calendars, curated feeds, and perfectly polished visuals weren't just for corporations anymore; they became the expectation for everyone. You, me, even the one-person shop down the street. Branding turned into a treadmill, and once you stepped on, you had to keep running or risk being told you "don't want it enough."

Key Takeaway: Branding turned into daily performance.

Stage Seven:
DEMOCRATISATION

And here we are. The gates are wide open and everyone's invited in. Over the last decade, branding has entered a whole new phase. Tools like Canva, Figma, and AI haven't made everyone world-class designers, but they've made branding more accessible, which is brilliant.

What once lived behind studio doors is now right there on your laptop, ready for anyone to play with. For a long time, looking professional was a signal that you had money. That's no longer true. Today, even a tiny startup or one-person business can look the part without spending a fortune.

Sure, a trained eye might spot a few rough edges, but honestly, only designers notice that stuff. Everyone else just sees a brand that looks the part and does the job.

And this shift matters. Because if a professional look is no longer rare, the real differentiator isn't the surface stuff: It's the reputation you build around the idea. That's what branding really is. And that's where designers come in. You shape how an idea is seen, trusted, and remembered. That's what makes you invaluable.

Key Takeaway: A professional look is easier to achieve. The value lies in shaping reputation.

So, my friends, there we are. You've got the foundation you need from the worst history teacher in the world—me. You've seen how branding wandered off track, and how it always circles back to the same truth.

Across history, one thing stays true. Reputation and perception sit at the heart of every brand. We trust what we recognise and follow the ideas that earn our confidence.

Now, let's move into the Ivory Tower mindset. This next one will get you thinking.

Chapter Two –

THE IVORY TOWER MINDSET

Somewhere along the way, brand building got locked in an ivory tower. Not by everyone, but by a mindset that's slowly crept in as the world around us changed.

As social media took off, as new tools popped up, and as creativity and design became more accessible for people to act on, a metaphorical tower began to rise. It wasn't built out of arrogance or greed; it was built out of fear. If the barrier to entry was falling, if anyone could suddenly download an app and start creating, what did that mean for the people who had studied, practiced, and invested years of their lives into the craft? It's not hard to see why some wanted to protect it, to build walls, to dig moats, to make the work feel harder to access.

That instinct is primal, and in many ways it makes perfect sense. When something you love feels threatened, your first reaction is to defend it. But that attempt to protect the craft ended up creating distance . . . distance between clients and designers, between pros and newcomers. What started as protection slowly turned into a divide between the work itself and the people who needed it most.

And here's the consequence no one saw coming . . . when design felt harder to reach, people didn't stop needing it. They just found their own way to do it. That's how alternatives are born. It reminds me of something Stephen Covey, the author of the classic book *The 7 Habits of Highly Effective People*, once said. He wrote:

"We are free to choose our actions, but we are not free to choose the consequences of those actions."

And that's exactly what happened here. The instinct to protect design was understandable, but the unintended consequence was a massive gap. Into that gap rushed a wave of tools, platforms, and technology that made design feel accessible again . . . not because people wanted to replace designers, but because people still needed design.

Social media has poured needless fuel on the fire. Suddenly, echo chambers popped up left, right, and centre, and debates over the tools we all used turned tribal. It became Adobe versus Canva, "real designer" versus "amateur." The software people used became their war paint, as if the program defined their value or creativity, or proved how good they were. And as we know, when things turn tribal, lines get drawn, sides get picked, and the actual purpose of design gets lost in the noise. Before you know it, someone's waving a sword around and you're left wondering what the battle was even about, and why someone on your side is wanting to harm you.

The reality is that creativity has never cared about tools or titles. Sure, there was a time when professional design tools were expensive, maybe a touch complicated, and only in the hands of trained designers. But that time has gone. Today, the tools are everywhere, and the difference is what you do with them, not whether you own them. Creativity still comes alive when you play, when you experiment, when you let the messy stuff out of your head and into the world, however scrappy it looks at first. Ideas are solved in your mind, not in your design software.

The danger of spending all your energy guarding the past is that you risk missing the future. Just ask Nokia. In the early 2000s, they were almost untouchable, selling hundreds of millions of mobile phones every year. Everyone I knew had one. But then Apple dropped the iPhone and BlackBerry made email mobile-friendly, and the whole game shifted. Phones stopped being about ringtones and those indestructible bricks you could launch across the room without a scratch, and suddenly it was all about touchscreens, apps, and slick software.

Nokia didn't move with it. They hid in their tower and protected what was. They kept improving their old keypad phones while the world was thumb-swiping into the future. By the time they tried to adapt, the crown had already been passed on.

And that's the big danger of the Ivory Tower mindset. It doesn't just shut people out; it keeps the people inside stuck protecting what was instead of exploring what could be.

Nobody's the villain here. Designers who fall into this mindset aren't acting out of malice; they're acting out of love for their craft. It's totally understandable. But if we don't call it out and make it real, the distance only grows, and I fear that distance can do more harm than good.

Lincoln Retreat 2024

Which brings us back to belonging.

Back in chapter 1, we talked about how belonging has always been at the heart of branding. The Ivory Tower mindset flips that belonging and starts to turn it into exclusion. Instead of design feeling like an open community, it starts to feel like a private club. A club with unspoken rules about who's "in" and who's "not ready yet." And when creativity is framed as a club instead of a community, everybody loses. Clients lose access. Designers lose opportunities. Businesses are never built.

So, this is my open-hearted message to the design community (and to anyone who proudly calls themselves a creative). Let's freaking stick together.

Tools aren't the point here. Neither are titles, degrees, or the way you were taught to design. What matters is the work, the ideas, the energy we bring.

Imagine a creative world where we can all express ourselves freely, with whatever background, process, or platform we happen to use, without anyone being judged as "less than" or "more than" because of it.

That's not about changing your software, your process, or your values. It's simply about choosing a different lens, one that sees the creative industry as stronger when we lift each other up. Because the truth is, we need each other. And the last thing we need is a divided creative community when we have every chance to build something better together.

The creative world is richer when more people play, not fewer. And the sooner we drop the Ivory Tower mindset, the sooner we can get back to what matters: the ideas, our expression, and that wonderful human connection.

Lincoln Design Co. Merch

Chapter Three –

THE CULT OF COMPLEXITY

I've used my fair share of fancy "design wordage" over the years.

I've dressed up simple things to sound impressive. I think we all have from time to time. So, I am writing this particular chapter as a reminder to myself as much as anything. If the Ivory Tower was all about mindset, then the Cult of Complexity is all about language.

Somewhere along the way, the words we used started to run away from us. As designers found themselves wearing more and more hats—part marketer, part advertiser, part web human, part strategist, sometimes part magician—the vocabulary got more complicated, too. We've always had a soft spot for words, and we're good at dreaming ideas up, making them sound tasty, delicious, even a little bit fantabulous. As the role grew, the words grew with it, until suddenly everything started sounding bigger and fancier than it really was . . . how very "Mad Men Theatre" of us.

I was right there with everyone else, trying to squeeze who I was into a neat little bio, cramming a whole career into two lines to try and position myself in the best way. I never really used Twitter myself, but I saw the challenge they set over there: Squash a big idea into a handful of characters and somehow make it land. That's when I started to notice things shifting. Language wasn't always about being clear anymore. Sometimes it was underthought, sometimes it was overthought, and a lot of the time it just ended up trying to be a little too clever for its own good. If you couldn't be clear, at least you could sound impressive.

That's how a simple "I design logos" suddenly felt a bit underwhelming. But swap it out for "I activate archetypal frameworks across multichannel ecosystems" and suddenly it sounded like you'd discovered fire. The funny thing is, half the time even the people saying this stuff don't really know what it means . . . and I'll admit, I wrote it and I have no clue.

The funny thing is, I believe that most of the language we use today, especially online across our websites and social media, isn't necessarily to impress clients. It's actually more about impressing our designer friends. And that's fine to a point—we all want a nod and a wink from our peers (belonging)—but it does create a bit of a problem. Because the more we write for each other, the less accessible it becomes for the people we're actually trying to help.

Language is one of the most powerful tools we've got in branding. Get it right, and it can build trust, shape a positive perception, and make people feel confident in your work. Get it wrong, and it can do the opposite . . . it creates confusion, doubt, and distance.

Think about it from both sides of the table. For a designer, language is how you demonstrate value. When you can explain your ideas clearly, whether that's in a meeting, on a call, on your website, or in a social media post, you make it easy for people to understand the depth of what you do.

It demonstrates that you know your craft, you know your process, and you know how to guide someone through it. That perception feeds reputation, and a positive reputation builds trust . . . and trust is what every brand is really built on. This is the good stuff we want!

But language can just as easily work against you. If you start leaning on words that sound clever but don't really mean anything, or worse, words you don't fully understand yourself, you plant the seeds of doubt. A client might see a perfectly wordsmithed post online and think, "Wow, this person sounds like they really know their stuff."

But then they get on a call, and the conversation doesn't line up with that first impression they had of you. When the online version of you doesn't quite match the real-life you, that's when little cracks start to show. People get a bit unsure, the trust wobbles, and suddenly they're wondering if they've backed the right horse. In simple terms, when what people think they're getting and what they actually get aren't lining up . . . that's where doubt sneaks in.

> **CONSISTENT, CONFIDENT LANGUAGE MAKES YOU SOUND RELIABLE.**

"MASTERY IS THE OWNERSHIP OF READY KNOWLEDGE, AND THEN THE CONCEPTUAL UNDERSTANDING OF HOW TO USE IT."

— Dr Benjamin Hardy

Willpower Doesn't Work (Balance 2018)

This is why language is such an anchor point in the Cult of Complexity. Because it isn't just about how we talk; it's about how we're understood. If the words we use are creating barriers instead of bridges, we're missing the whole point. Clients don't hire designers to be impressed by jargon. They hire designers to help make sense of an idea and bring it into the world.

There's a quote I came across many moons ago that reads:

"Mastery is the ownership of ready knowledge, and then the conceptual understanding of how to use it."
Make It Stick: The Science of Successful Learning
(Belknap Press 2014)

To me, this means that when you really know something, you don't need to overly dress it up. You can explain it in a way that lands. You can take something that feels complicated on the surface and make it feel simple, obvious, and approachable.

Language works the same way. When you're confident in your craft, you don't need to try too hard to "sound the part." You can strip things back and explain them clearly, in a way that makes people lean in and trust what you're saying . . . and selling.

That's the real power of language in branding. It isn't about looking clever; it's about creating trust. The clearer you are, the easier it is for people to believe in you, invest in you, and build with you. Get the words right, and you're not just shaping perception; you're shaping all of your future opportunities. And that, my friends, is the good stuff.

Chapter Four –

THE DEMOCRATISATION DILEMMA

What Happens When There's Access Without Guidance?

One of the most exciting things about being alive right now is that anyone can design. The gates are wide open, the tools are friendly, and people everywhere are discovering ways to express their creativity that simply weren't possible before. That isn't a minor shift . . . it's a full-blown revolution, and I'm absolutely here for it.

For me, creativity has always been more than work . . . it's where I'm at my happiest. When I'm sketching, playing with ideas, or making something with my hands, I feel calmer, more present, more like my good old self. It's not about whether the end result is "good," it's about the process of making something from nothing, that calming flow you slip into. That's the space where I feel at home, and it's something I'm nurturing in my son, too, because I know firsthand the joy and confidence it can build.

And the science backs that up. Psychologists have shown that even short bursts of creative activity can reduce stress, lift your mood, and boost your confidence. Creativity doesn't just make things . . . it makes people happier. It builds resilience, strengthens self-belief, and gives you that reminder that **you can** do anything.

That's why I celebrate the democratisation of design so much. It's not just that more people can create, it's that they get to tap back into that childlike creative space we all had once. Remember, we were all born creative . . . life just has a habit of knocking it out of us. The democratisation gives people the chance to find that spark again. To feel the joy and benefits of making.

Take my mother-in-law, Di. She's fallen head over heels for Canva. One minute she's making labels for her jams and chutneys, the next she's designing graphics for her leather projects, and the next she's spinning up artwork for one of her 243 side hustles (I've lost count, and I'll probably get a clip round the ear for saying that—love you, Di). And I think that's brilliant. That's creativity as play. That's design being let loose without barriers. And it makes me smile every time I see it . . . or receive some jam.

DILEMMA!

the Democratisation Dilemma

But (and you knew there was a but coming) . . . freedom always has a flip side.

Because when everyone can design, the world fills up super fast. Logos start to look alike. Content begins to blur. Brands start to feel interchangeable. You see the same chunky fonts, the same cheerful illustrations, the same candy-coloured gradients, recycled and reused until it's hard to tell who's who.

The dilemma isn't that access exists. The dilemma is what happens when access collides head-on with a lack of intention.

When tools are this easy, it's tempting to create just because you can. A post because, well . . . it's Tuesday. A new logo because a template looked like it had a better vibe. A colour tweak because this week's trending shade is lemon fuzz or peach popsicle. Each decision feels harmless, but stacked together, they create a lot of noise. Instead of building recognition, the brand being built starts to drift.

AND IN A NOISY WORLD, DRIFTING IS THE FASTEST WAY TO DISAPPEAR.

Now, let's be incredibly clear here . . . there's nothing wrong with creating for the sake of creating. My mother-in-law, Di, isn't building a commercial brand. She's not trying to scale her leather goods or sell jars of chutney to the masses. She makes things because it's fun, because she enjoys it, and because she likes things to look a little bit pretty before she gives them away. That's creativity and design as pure play and expression.

The issue comes when people step into the world of commercial brand building. Branding is about consistency and about building evidence and perception over time. And that's where access without intention can backfire. If everyone is reaching for the same visual assets or changing their design decisions like the wind, the result isn't a unique identity . . . it's sameness and confusion.

We all know that our clients are already playing around with Canva, they're starting to dabble more in AI, and they're grabbing templates like they're going out of fashion. That's the world we live in now, and it's a world packed with chances for us to step in and bring a bit of direction to all that enthusiasm. I am a big believer that we're needed more now than ever.

The rise of DIY design doesn't spell fewer jobs for designers; it actually means more opportunities. More people are experimenting, which means there are more people who need guidance, who are hungry for clarity, and who are looking for someone to help them. The problem has never really been access, because the tools are everywhere now. The real gap is between access and intention, and that is exactly where we as designers get to plant our (well-designed) flag.

Our role is to lead the future design world and creative community. To become the guide, the mentor, the art director who shows clients how to channel their creativity with purpose. To help them make the right decisions. We're not here to get in the way. We're here to empower, we're here to hand people a compass and show them how far they can go . . . and to make sure they're heading in the right direction.

MY MOTHER-IN-LAW, DI, ON HER 243RD SIDE HUSTLE, KNITTING FOR ROCCO

So, this is where we as brand builders step into the spotlight. Tools have given everyone the ability to design, but they haven't given everyone the ability to think like a designer. That's the part only we can do . . . all the intentional-thought goodness. The stuff that turns creativity into consistency, and consistency into trust.

That's the opportunity in front of us, friends . . . to stop thinking like executors and start showing up as the creative guides we are, or, as I like to call myself, a Brand Host. For me, a Brand Host sets the environment for ideas to take shape, guiding and supporting people with clarity and intention so their raw ideas turn into real brands. That's the role we get to own, and it's needed now more than ever.

What I am actually most excited about is that once you've got the Five Idea Keys and the MVB mindset in your arsenal, you're not just building brands . . . you're building relationships. This is something you can give to the clients who aren't "ready" yet, the ones who can't afford the big process but still need clarity at the start. It becomes your friendship builder, your relationship builder, your network builder. Because when their idea grows, when the money starts coming in, and when they're ready to level up their brand, there will only be one person they trust to guide them—you.

I know you want the same thing I do . . . more ideas turning into brands that are built with intention, not blind panic. Because when that happens, it's good for everyone. More successful brands in the world means more meaningful work for designers like us. And this leads me onto the next obstacle I have seen in our design world, the rush to look "legit" . . . let's move on to panic branding.

Chapter Five –

PANIC BRANDING

Panic branding is a bit like drunk texting your ex after eight tequilas. In the moment, it feels bold, exciting, maybe even like the smartest move of your life. But by the next morning, you're staring at the mess, head in hands, wondering why you thought any of it was a good idea.

Branding in panic works the same way. You're not building with a plan; you're just reacting, lobbing things at the wall to see what sticks and convincing yourself it's progress until the regret kicks in. Fear's in the mix; so is comparison, and then comes that desperate urge to look like a "real" brand before you've even worked out what "real" actually means.

So, the decisions come fast and frantic: a quick logo here, a shiny website there, maybe even a new service or product you're not completely sure about but feels good in the moment. From the outside, it looks like you're building momentum. But underneath, you know it's shaky, more like a house of cards than a solid foundation. Fine until the slightest breeze comes along and blows the whole thing over.

Trust me . . . I know this from experience. Back in 2012, I launched a clothing company called Sometimes Square. You've never heard of it, and that's because it tanked almost immediately. Not because the idea was terrible, but because I panic-branded the life out of it. I spent weeks sketching and developing a logo system, registered a trademark, bought a domain, designed a slick website, even ordered custom-woven tags for the T-shirts. All of that before I'd sold a single tee. On paper, it looked like momentum. In reality, it was blind panic . . . panic to look legitimate, panic to keep up with everyone else flogging merch, panic to convince myself I wasn't wasting my time. The irony, of course, is that I ended up wasting loads of it anyway.

That's the trap with panic branding. It rarely comes from bad intentions; in fact, most of the time it comes from the best ones. You want to move forward. You want to show the world you're building something. You want to feel like you're not falling behind. And your brain, being a perfectly normal human brain, would always rather give you the wrong answer right now than leave you sitting in the discomfort of having no answer at all.

This is where the psychology kicks in, and it's the part that should actually make you feel better. Panic branding isn't proof you're stupid (unless we're counting that tequila text). It's proof you're human, because our brains are wired to behave exactly like this.

SOME OF THE BIGGEST CULPRITS ARE:

Loss aversion:
A bias that makes us fear losses more than we enjoy gains. Psychologists have found that losing a thing feels about twice as painful as winning that same thing feels good. That's why seeing someone else get ahead doesn't just feel like ***their*** win—it feels like ***your*** loss, and your brain starts panicking.
Example: Losing $10 hurts a lot more than finding $10 feels good.

Uncertainty intolerance:
Most of us find "not knowing" harder to handle than getting the wrong answer. The brain wants closure, even if it's false, because sitting in ambiguity feels unbearable. That's why rushing to put a logo on your idea feels better than leaving it undefined, even if you're not ready yet.
Example: It's easier to throw up a quick brand mark than to admit you don't know what you're building.

Performance mindset (the halo effect):
A bias where one good impression makes us believe everything else must be good, too. In branding, visuals carry this weight: If it ***looks*** polished, we assume the business is strong. Social media makes this even worse, rewarding appearances over reality.
Example: A slick Instagram grid convinces people the brand is thriving, even if sales are nonexistent.

Busywork comfort (avoidance coping):
A strategy where we bury ourselves in easy, low-risk tasks to avoid facing harder or scarier ones. It feels productive, but it's really procrastination in disguise. In branding, this shows up as endless fiddling with fonts or layouts instead of tackling the bigger strategic questions.
Example: Spending hours tweaking your colour palette feels like progress, but it doesn't actually move the brand forward.

When you put all these instincts together—the fear of losing, the discomfort of not knowing, the belief that looking good means being good, and the comfort of busywork—it's no wonder panic branding shows up so easily.

But panic branding isn't the real enemy. The actual fire is something underneath it, something louder, sneakier, and harder to shake. I call it *the Rush*.

THE RUSH

The Rush is that smooth-talking voice in your head that loves to stir the pot. It tells you you're already behind, that the window of opportunity is closing, that everyone else is sprinting while you're still tying your shoelaces. It doesn't come barging in, shouting orders . . . it slips in quietly, disguised as "productivity." It tells you the only way forward is to hustle harder, move faster, and make snap decisions, otherwise you're not really making meaningful progress.

In the moment, it feels spot-on. You tell yourself you're grinding, putting in the hours, doing what designers are "supposed" to do. But the Rush doesn't care if you're moving forward or just running in circles . . . it just wants you moving. Any direction will do. And in the chaos, you end up swapping what matters for what's urgent, trading clarity for more confusion, and turning real progress into the kind of frantic busywork that looks impressive but . . . doesn't actually get you anywhere. We've all churned out enough pointless content for the algorithmic overlords to prove that one true.

I used to fall for the Rush all the time. In doing so, it quietly stripped away the things I actually needed most: my direction, my clarity, and, more often than I'd like to admit, my happiness. And the truth is, it never fully goes away. Even now it still sneaks back in, masquerading as "effort," but I've learned how to ignore the cheeky trickster . . . most of the time.

You'll know the Rush has you when you catch yourself doing things like:

- **Rushing to redesign your website just because a friend or peer has launched a shiny new one.**
- **Churning out content not because you've got something to say, but because everyone else seems to be posting daily.**
- **Copying trends instead of defining your own style, blending into the crowd to feel safe rather than standing out.**
- **Saying yes to work that doesn't fit who you are or what you value, simply because "everyone else" would jump at it.**
- **Chasing quick wins because you see others celebrating them online, instead of putting in the slower, compounding work that lasts.**

If you've done any of those things, that's not failure. It just means you cared enough to try. We live in a world that worships speed and visibility over real substance. The louder the noise gets, the more urgent everything feels. And our brains, bless them, are built to follow the crowd . . . you've no doubt heard of the term *groupthink*. It's a psychological phenomenon where people suppress doubts and go along with the majority, even when they sense something's off, just to avoid standing out.

And it's not just designers, freelancers, or small studios who get caught up in it. Some of the biggest, most celebrated companies on the planet have fallen for it, too, with consequences far bigger than a wobbly website or a wasted logo effort.

Think Fyre Festival, a so-called luxury music festival that turned into a disaster-relief campsite. Think the 2008 financial crash, fuelled by blind optimism and copycat behaviour. Think WeWork's IPO, hyped to a $47 billion valuation before investors realised the model was broken.

And then there's Theranos, maybe the clearest example of the Rush and groupthink colliding on a massive scale. Elizabeth Holmes promised the world that hundreds of blood tests could be run in minutes, on a single drop of blood. It was a story almost too good to resist. The branding was great, the pitch was magnetic, and investors lined up with their wallets wide open. At one point, the company was valued at $9 billion.

But . . . the technology never actually worked. People inside the company knew it, but the momentum was so strong that nobody wanted to be the one to hit the brakes. Not because they were stupid or evil, but because once the train was moving, everyone assumed someone else had already checked the truth. That's the Rush at its most dangerous. It doesn't just waste time or money . . . it warps judgment so completely that even smart people, with all the resources in the world, stop asking the obvious questions.

This should actually make us as designers feel a lot better. If billionaires, ex-presidents, and global investors can get swept up in the Rush, then, of course, our clients can, too. And that's important to remember. When they come to us asking for things on impossible timelines, or demanding a "quick logo," it's not because they don't respect our work. It's because they've been conditioned by society to believe that faster is always better.

And hey—the next time they do, you can smile and say, "You're panic branding."

The Rush is everywhere. It shows up in the myth of overnight success, in the obsession with follower counts, in the promise that the next big client will magically make you "legit." Now that you can see the Rush for what it is, you don't have to get dragged along by it. You don't have to buy into the panic or feed it; you can slow it down, laugh at it a little, and choose to build things properly.

So, with that in mind, let's have some fun with it. Let's ignore the Rush for a moment, flip the lens, and look at the surefire ways to really mess things up.

Welcome to Burn Baby Burn:
10 Ways to Burn Your Brand.

10 WAYS TO BURN YOUR BRAND

One of the most useful mental models I've ever come across is Charlie Munger's inversion principle. Instead of asking, "How do we succeed?" he flips it to, "How do we fail?"

When I first read that, it was a lightbulb moment. I started using inversion everywhere . . . in design, in branding, in deciding which ideas to run with and which ones to pop in the bin. Rather than focusing on success, I pause and ask: "How could this go wrong?" Then I work backward to avoid it.

And here's why this matters for us as designers. Most clients are in the Rush. They are chasing speed, money, hype. They think that if they just "look legit," they'll be legit. If we don't stop and ask, "How could this go wrong?" on their behalf, who will? That's what makes us creative partners, and it's a great way to frame your concerns.

Branding is the perfect place for inversion. If you only chase the shiny "how to succeed" advice, you miss the obvious mistakes that quietly burn brands to the ground. And, let's be honest, we've all lit a few matches ourselves.

So, let's flip it. Here are the fastest ways to set a brand on fire . . . and not in the good way.

---

1. Confusing speed with progress:
Moving quickly without clarity creates work, not progress.

2. Polishing the outside and ignoring the inside:
Strong visuals cannot compensate for a weak or undefined idea.

3. Copying what's working for someone else:
Following trends or competitors only makes you harder to notice.

4. Saying yes to panic deadlines:
Rushed work leaves no room for considered design thinking.

5. Mistaking busywork for brand work:
Endless tweaks without decisions waste energy and slow everything down.

6. Outsourcing the hard thinking:
A vague brief or lack of clarity makes it impossible to design effectively.

7. Chasing validation instead of a reputation:
Approval and likes are not the same as building a trusted brand.

8. Believing the hype:
Loud attention does not guarantee substance or sustainability.

9. Building in isolation:
Keeping work to yourself prevents the feedback and testing that make it stronger.

10. Forgetting that ideas need time:
Rushing skips the space needed for ideas to develop properly.

Every designer I know, myself included, has fallen into at least one of these traps. The difference now is that we have inversion. It helps us spot the mistakes earlier and catch ourselves before we start spiralling into them.

That's the value. Not just making things look good, but building with enough awareness to stop brands from burning before they've even started.

Chapter Six –

THE SOCIAL MEDIA CIRCUS

Back in 1921, the biologist William Beebe was trekking through the South American rainforest when he spotted something unusual. On the jungle floor, thousands of army ants were marching in a giant circle, a loop stretching over 1,200 feet (366 m) around. Each ant took more than two hours to complete a single lap. At first it looked impressive, almost choreographed. Then, Beebe realised that they weren't going anywhere.

Scientists later called this phenomenon the *ant death spiral*, which is a rare glitch where the pheromone trail loops back on itself.

Every ant is convinced it's on the right path, but really, they're just looping endlessly with no way out. Round and round they go for hours, sometimes days, until eventually they collapse from exhaustion.

That, to me, is social media in a nutshell.

> **FROM THE OUTSIDE, IT LOOKS COORDINATED. EVERYONE'S MOVING, POSTING, GROWING, AND SHARING THEIR BEST BITS. IT LOOKS LIKE PROGRESS, BUT MOST OF THE TIME IT'S JUST MOTION WITHOUT ANY REAL DIRECTION.**

Designers following designers, brands copying brands, all of us caught in the loop of showing up simply because everyone else is showing up. It can feel like the "smart" thing to do, but just like those ants, we're often just stuck in a loop that doesn't end anywhere useful.

Here's what I've noticed. Whenever I get sucked into the spiral, there are usually two things at play. First, it distracts the hell out of me . . . and pulls me away from the work I should be doing. And second, it gets me comparing myself to everybody else. Those two together? That's the cocktail that messes with your head.

ENGINE ONE: DISTRACTION — THE SCATTERER

Social media is the great scatterer of creative focus. It doesn't politely ask for your attention; it fractures it. Every ping, every like, every new feature slices your day into smaller and smaller pieces. Instead of doing the deep work on an idea, you find yourself doomscrolling, watching a load of things, from a load of people you don't even follow.

The danger here is that branding doesn't really survive the scattering. Your ideas need space to properly form. Your reputation is built on consistency, and the more your attention gets pulled in ten different directions, the shakier your brand's foundation becomes. That's the first trap of the spiral . . . it drags you away from the craft and convinces you that firing out another post is the same as making progress.

And sure, posting every day can look like consistency, but there's a world of difference between filling a feed and building a reputation. All that time you burn on doomscrolling or chasing the vanity metrics could be spent on things that actually feed your creativity—focusing on curating your design taste, building friendships with new people, reading something that sparks an idea, or just letting your brain breathe for a little bit. That's the stuff that makes your work stand out. Endless posting doesn't feed your brand; it runs your brand ragged. Trust me, I've been there, often still find myself there, and I've got all the T-shirts to prove it.

ENGINE TWO: COMPARISON — THE SHRINKER

If distraction scatters your focus, comparison is the shrinker of your identity. Psychologists call it *upward social comparison*. That's the fancy term for what happens when you scroll the feed, see someone else doing better, and suddenly, your own work feels smaller. Maybe it's a designer landing a "dream client," or someone pulling in more likes on a project that doesn't even look that special to you. It doesn't matter how much you know it's just the highlight reel . . . in the moment, it gets under your skin.

And I want you to know, you're not alone in that. I've spoken to thousands of designers over the years, and every single one of us has felt this way at some point. It's normal. The scroll shrinks us all from time to time. For designers, that shrinking often takes a specific shape . . . you see what's trending and feel the urge to bend your style to match it, or you hear how others tell their story and start tweaking your own to fit. Bit by bit, you shave off the edges of your own voice until it blends neatly with everyone else's.

The result is what I call the Great Copy-and-Paste Effect. Suddenly everyone's using the same fonts, pumping out the same templates, posting the same "top 10" carousels, and even laying out their case studies in the exact same way. Scroll for five minutes and it all starts to blur together.

And look, from the outside it can feel comforting . . . like you're part of the club, ticking the right boxes, keeping up. But what it's really doing is sanding down the very things that make you different. The spiral tricks you into swapping originality for safety. Instead of leaning into the quirks, edges, and ideas that actually make you stand out, you end up chasing what feels comfortable and approved. Safe feels good in the moment . . . but safe rarely builds a brand that anyone remembers.

Put distraction and comparison together, and you've got the full-blown trap. One pulls you away from the craft. The other convinces you that you're not enough (like being at school again). So, you post more, scroll more, copy more, until your brand starts to look, sound, and feel like everyone else's.

This is also the point where our friend perception sneaks in as both the power and the problem. Social media proves every single day how powerful perception can be. A designer can look successful online long before they have any real evidence. With the right filters, the right tone, the right language, you can project success instantly. That's the game the platforms reward. Perception matters because it gets you noticed. But without the evidence to back it up, it's incredibly brittle. Clients might come through the door because of perception, but they stay, and they refer others, because of evidence.

The social media spiral can push us into a mindset where perception comes first and we just hope the evidence will follow later. It makes us feel like we need to look more capable than we actually are, and if we just keep showing up, maybe the proof will catch up. But that's not really a brand with strong foundations. Don't get me wrong, perception is incredibly powerful—it gets people to notice you—but evidence is what makes them trust you and stay with you.

THE REAL MAGIC HAPPENS WHEN THE TWO WORK TOGETHER.

This chapter isn't about telling you that you should or shouldn't post on social media. There are plenty of positives. It's a brilliant way to show your work. It's a brilliant way to build community. It's a fantastic asset for reputation building if used the right way. It forces you to get better at explaining what you do. And yes, it's a powerful tool for building perception—and as we know, perception is an important force when it comes to branding.

What I do want to make you aware of are the traps: distraction and comparison. They're easy to fall into, and I know because I've fallen into them myself. For a long time, I thought I was moving forward, but really I was just busy, visible, but not heading toward the things I actually cared about. It left me a little drained, chasing the wrong things like views and likes rather than things like more time outside with my son.

That was the moment I had to step back and ask myself a bigger question: What does success actually look like for me? Not the version sold on the feed, but the version that fits the kind of life I want to build. Once I figured that out, social media stopped being the driver and became just another tool I could use to support that bigger picture of helping people design their own way.

And that brings me nicely to another cheeky mindset hack that helped me focus on *my* version of success as a designer and business owner. Honestly, it was a huge brain expander for me, and I'm excited to share it with you. It came from my great friend Thad, and it's called Lifestyle Pricing.

THAD'S LIFESTYLE PRICING

Over the years, I've realised that chasing "more" for the sake of it doesn't really energise me. More clients, more money, more numbers on a screen . . . it all sounds impressive, but it doesn't get me out of bed in the morning. What does? Time with my son, my wife, and my friends. Space to explore my own creativity and ideas. Room to enjoy the life I've built, not just keep pushing for the next milestone.

My buddy Thad, who's been a good mate for years, introduced me to an idea that flipped the way I think about business and life. He calls it ***Lifestyle Pricing.***

The principle is simple. Instead of chasing the internet's obsession with "seven figures" or listening to the noise about scaling endlessly, you start with the life you actually want and build backward from there.

Here's the way Thad breaks it down:

1. **Define the lifestyle:** What does a great life look like for you? Not for Instagram. For you.
2. **Calculate the cost:** Work out the number that supports that life—dreams, bills, essentials.
3. **Balance work and life:** Decide how much you want to work and how much you want to live.
4. **Set the price:** Take that cost and divide it by your ideal working days. That's your real rate.
5. **Widen the gap:** Cut unnecessary expenses to create more freedom.
6. **Match services to price:** Shape your offers so they line up with that rate.
7. **Choose the right clients:** Work with people who value what you do at the price you've set.
8. **Build compounding assets:** Books, courses, products—things that keep earning when you're not.
9. **Invest in yourself:** Learn new skills that let you charge more for less of your time.

When you start working this way, you stop measuring yourself against someone else's scoreboard. You stop chasing numbers that don't matter. You give yourself back your time, you build things that keep working even when you're not, and you shape your work to fit around your life—not the other way round.

Lifestyle first. Then the money. Then the clients.

If you're the kind of person who likes to dig deeper, I've put together a handy resource folder with all the tools, links, and extras from this book. Nice and simple, all in one place. You'll find it by scanning the QR code below.

~~CLIENT → MONEY → LIFESTYLE~~

LIFESTYLE → MONEY → CLIENT

Chapter Seven –

BRANDING'S BOOBY TRAPS: A RECAP

So there we are, friends. That's the little tour of where branding sometimes goes a bit off track. It's not the definitive history, not the final word . . . just my take on the patterns I've seen over the years. Hopefully it's given you a decent pair of gumpf goggles (my nickname for the filter that helps me spot the nonsense) to see the traps a bit quicker and steer around them.

It's not about feeling guilty, because we've all fallen into these traps at some point. I've fallen for every single one of them, more than once. The rushed logos, the panicked content creation, the chasing of success that left me halfway up a ladder I never wanted to climb. If you've done the same, welcome to the club . . . it just means you're a designer being human. (And that's a great thing.)

The point is awareness, so don't beat yourself up. Pop the gumpf goggles on, have a chuckle at the chaos, and use it as fuel to make better choices moving forward.

HERE'S THE QUICK MAP OF WHAT WE'VE JUST WALKED THROUGH:

- **The Ivory Tower** — When we try to protect the craft by building walls instead of bridges. The instinct is natural, but the real strength comes when we invite people in. Guiding more people is how design grows.

- **The Cult of Complexity** — When language turned into theatre. Jargon might sound impressive, but clarity is what actually builds trust. The more simply you can explain the work, the more powerful it becomes.

- **The Democratisation Dilemma** — When access meets the intention gap. Tools gave everyone the ability to make, but not the ability to think like a designer. That's where we come in. Our role is to guide, to show how creativity can have purpose as well as be playful.

- **The Rush** — That itch to move faster just to keep up. But momentum without clarity rarely lasts. The real win is slowing down long enough to see direction, then moving with forward with confidence.

- **Panic Branding** — The scramble to look "legit" before the idea is ready. It can feel like progress, but often it's just busywork in disguise. When we start with clarity, every decision builds on a foundation that can actually hold.

- **The Social Media Circus** — Distraction and comparison dressed up as consistency. The lesson here is simple: Perception gets you noticed, but evidence earns you trust. When you focus on both, your brand has real staying power.

All of these traps might look different on the surface, but they share the same effect: They get in the way. They block your ideas from taking shape, they weaken your own brand when you fall into them, and they just as easily derail the brands you're building for clients.

And that's the real lesson worth carrying forward. Once you know these traps exist, you don't have to fear them. In the words of Charlie Munger, look at how things fail, then choose the opposite. Here's what that looks like for us:

GUARDING → GUIDING

JARGON → CLARITY

TOOLS → TASTE

SPEED → DIRECTION

PERFORMANCE → FOUNDATIONS

FEED → EVIDENCE

That inversion is where progress as a brand really begins. It's not about perfection, and it's definitely not about never slipping up again. It's about recognising the patterns, catching yourself a little quicker each time, and choosing differently when they show up.

And now we get to the exciting part.

Now, we step into section two, where we really dive into what branding is all about. I'll show you how I approach building brands in the studio, and we'll hear from some of the best brand builders on the planet, who will share their own wisdom. We'll look at the process, the craft, the creativity, and we'll have a lot of fun doing it. Expect plenty of ideas, plenty of visuals, and hopefully a few lightbulb moments along the way.

Grab a sip or two before we begin . . . then bed in for some proper brand thinking, no-fluff style.

NO BULLSHIT
BY JAMES

SECTION TWO

MAKING THE COMPLEX SIMPLE

In this next section, we're going to look at the branding process in a whole new light. The goal here is to give you a new perspective on the things that build a brand and make them last. We'll start by breaking down what branding really is and dig into how reputation actually works. Then, I'll walk you through my DDD process, the same one I've used for years in the studio to help people bring their ideas into the world in a way that will make them last.

We will also be diving into some delicious case studies, hearing from some of the best studios in the world. It will be a feast for the eyes and the brain, and after we are done with this section, you'll have a new lens to share with your clients that will help you articulate your value and build your own brands with super-duper clarity.

INTO THE
WOODS
LOVE
WAY

Chapter Eight -

WHAT IS BRANDING, REALLY?

We're designers. We care about colour, detail, grids, kerning, the whole beautiful barrage of creative decisions that make things come alive. We sweat the tiny pixels, obsess over the craft, and take real pride in the work. But branding has always been bigger than the visuals we make. It's the stories we help shape, the behaviours we influence, the trust our work earns over time. Every design choice, from the way something looks to how it speaks to how it shows up in the world, is part of a much larger picture.

And when you stand back far enough to see that picture clearly, you realise what all of it is really building toward: reputation. And the best way to understand reputation? Start with your friends.

Think about the people you've got in your life. Your crew. The ones you grab a beer with after a long week or call when you need to vent about a project or relationship gone sideways. I'm sure a few names pop up straight away. Every single one of them carries a bit of a reputation, whether they know it or not. You probably don't even notice it happening, but over time you've built a little internal scoreboard for each of them. Who shows up. Who flakes. Who makes you laugh so hard you want to pee. Who disappears when you need them most.

You didn't plan to keep score—none of us do. But slowly, through all those moments you've created together—the good ones, the bad ones, the random late-night chats—you've formed a picture of who they are to you. And that picture quietly shapes how you treat them, what you expect from them, and when you call on them next.

There's the friend you'd call in your darkest moment. The one who always shows up, no matter the hour, no matter the drama. They've earned your trust so many times that you don't even hesitate. You know they'll answer. You know they'll be there.

Then there's the fun one. The mate you invite out when you need to blow off steam. You know the night will be full of laughs, stories, and maybe a little chaos. They're not the person you'd trust with something delicate, but if you want a good time, they're top of the list.

And then there are the wonderfully disorganised ones. The friend you adore, but you'd never trust with the early morning airport run when you are going on holiday. They'll either show up late, mix up the day, or realise halfway there that the car's out of fuel. You know the drill. Planning and punctuality aren't really their thing, but their heart is solid gold.

You didn't sit down and analyse all this. You didn't consciously decide what categories to put your friends in. Over time, through experiences and interactions, they built a reputation in your mind. That reputation shapes how you think about them and what role they play in your life.

And that, in its simplest form, is how branding works.

A brand is a recognisable reputation.

That was the clearest way I've ever heard it described, and I'm not going to take credit for it. It actually came up as a passing comment from a brilliant friend of mine, trusted brand brother Kevin Finn. We were chatting, as we often do, about the strange world of branding and how much of it comes down to human behaviour that often goes unnoticed.

I've always known that reputation plays a massive role in brand building as it's something I've spent nearly twenty years working on. But when I heard Kevin say this, I jumped on a call with him straight after and said, "Mate, I need to put that in my next book. Are you cool with that?" And in classic, kind, and calm Kevin style, he just said, "Yes friend, I'd love that . . . we came up with it together."

Kevin is one of those friends you can message at any hour with a half-formed theory, and I know he'll always throw something thoughtful back. Even though I'm in the UK and he is in Australia, I'll send him things like, "What do you think about this new framework?" or "Can true authenticity even exist in a personal brand?" And sure enough, he always replies. Thanks for the continued friendship, Kevin.

So, if a brand is a recognisable reputation, then branding is how you shape and share that reputation on purpose. It's how you show up, how you behave, and how you communicate. All of it shapes what people come to believe about you.

There are really two sides to reputation building. The first happens naturally; it's the organic stuff that forms over time through what people do and how they show up. Think back to Rocco in the intro. The second is the intentional side—the kind we design on purpose. Both matter, but in this book, we'll mostly focus on the intentional, commercial side of reputation building, helping clients shape how they're seen, build trust, and earn their place in the world.

The sweet spot is when the two align with truth and humanness. That's when the real magic starts to happen. But to keep things simple, let's break it down:

Reputation – The collective belief people hold about you.

Brand – The recognisable reputation you build over time.

Branding – The process of shaping, expressing, and proving that reputation.

Think of these three as our ground floor. Everything else we'll cover in this book builds on top of this.

For me, this is exactly why the process of branding matters so much. It's about taking ownership of how you're seen instead of letting other people decide for you. Branding gives you the power to choose your own box, to decorate it in a way that feels true, and to make sure what people think about you actually lines up with who you are. When you keep showing up consistently and honestly, you build the good stuff: trust. And trust is the single most important thing any brand can have. When people trust your brand, they feel confident choosing you again and again.

Branding matters now more than ever because, let's be honest, the world is very, very loud. Everyone's busy, everyone's distracted, and we're all hit with more choices than we can possibly process. That's where good branding steps in. It cuts through the noise and helps people make sense of it all. It gives them a quick shortcut, and you know now that we humans love a shortcut, to know who and what they can actually trust. It's how someone can spot your name, your work, or your words and instantly feel something, a moment of recognition that says, "Yeah, this is for me."

Another thing worth remembering is that branding isn't just for the outside world. It's not only about how customers see you or why they choose you. It's just as important for the people inside the room, the ones building, designing, writing, and making decisions every day. When a brand is clear, it keeps everyone on the same page. It helps teams move in the same direction, gives designers a stronger brief, and makes collaborations and partnerships easier to start and sustain. If everyone has alignment, then it's much easier and faster to get to where you want to go—everyone is pulling in the same direction.

In simple terms, branding is never really finished. It's about looking after the thing you've built and helping others do the same. It's showing teams how to use the work properly, setting up simple systems so things stay consistent, and leaving clear signposts so good decisions keep happening even when you are not there.

That is why you, as a designer, are so damn valuable. If you can learn to explain this clearly, in real human language, you are golden.

That's why learning to talk about branding in this way is such a game-changer. If you can explain to a client that your job isn't just to make things look good, but to shape how people trust them, that's where the real power lives. You stop being seen as the person who just makes things look good and start being recognised as someone who creates meaning, a creative partner who helps people see clearly. That's when clients start listening differently.

So now that we understand what branding is, let's dig into how reputations are actually built. Because knowing the idea is one thing . . . building it with intention is a whole different ballgame. If you're anything like me, you probably like having something visual to check in with, a way to see the invisible work made visible. Something you can use to guide your clients and yourself toward more consistent, meaningful results.

That's where the Reputation Grid comes in. It's a simple way to see where reputations grow strong, where they wobble, and how to keep them steady. It will help you design brands that don't just look great, but also earn trust through evidence, behaviour, and experience . . . this is going to be fun.

"IF YOU DON'T POSITION YOURSELF, YOU WILL BE POSITIONED."

— Sasha Strauss

Chapter Nine -

THE REPUTATION GRID

If you've made it this far, firstly, congratulations (I do like to waffle on). Secondly, you already know how much of branding comes down to reputation, how people think and feel about you, and the trust that grows or fades from what you do every day. But knowing that is one thing; seeing how it actually works is another.

For years, I used to describe reputation as this fuzzy thing that just "builds over time." But that's not very helpful when you're trying to make real choices, or when a client asks, "How do we actually build trust?" or "Where should we focus our efforts?"

That's why I created the Reputation Grid.

It's a simple visual that shows where trust really comes from and how the different parts of a reputation depend on each other. You can see a visual of the grid here.

The grid breaks a brand's reputation down into four parts:

- **Integrity: Do your actions actually match your words and values?**
- **Competence: Can people rely on you to do what you say you'll do?**
- **Community: Who's in your corner helping share and shape your story?**
- **Narrative: How is that story told? How believable does it feel to others?**

Together, these form the foundation of any strong reputation. And holding them steady, like glue, is consistency.

Within each of those four areas, there has to be evidence—evidence of integrity, competence, community, and narrative. Because without proof, trust doesn't stand a chance. People believe what they see, not just what they're told. That's our job as designers: to help our clients make those truths visible. When the evidence lines up with the story, trust grows. And when all four parts work together consistently, that's when a reputation really starts to gain traction.

The beauty of this model is that it doesn't add complexity; it brings clarity. Once you understand these four parts, you can start to design for them in your work, your process, and the way you guide clients.

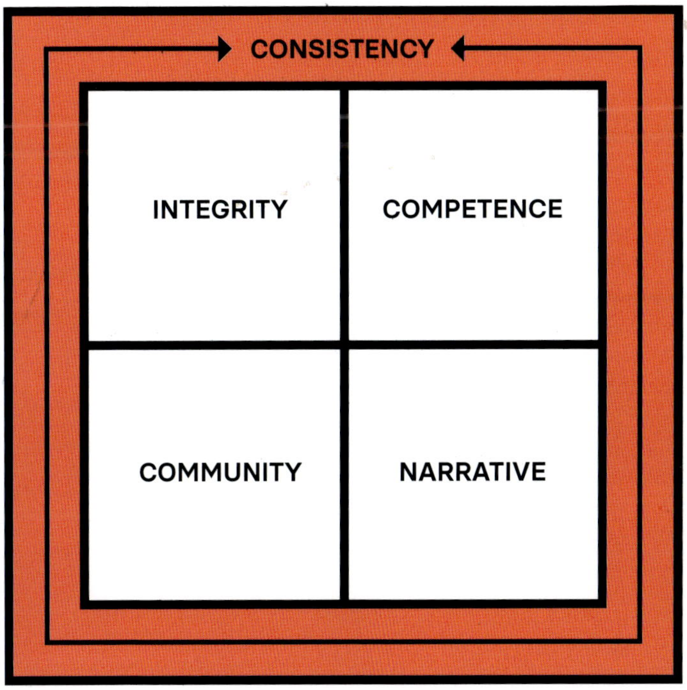

INTEGRITY

Integrity is where every strong reputation begins. It means doing what you say you'll do, even when no one's watching.

You can have smart strategy, clever messaging, and stunning visuals, but if people sense a gap between your words and actions, trust disappears fast. Integrity shows up in the details, fair pricing, transparent communication, keeping promises, owning mistakes. People notice the little things more than you think, and they add up fast.

For designers, this means aligning what a brand says with what it shows. If a client claims honesty or transparency, the design should prove it.

Takeaway: Integrity isn't about perfection. It's about honesty and proof.

COMMUNITY

Community is the company you keep, the people who help shape, share, and spread your reputation. Clients, collaborators, followers, friends, fans.

Reputation travels through people. The right community amplifies your message; the wrong one erodes it. Every testimonial, collaboration, or shout-out is proof of who's in your corner.

For designers, your community is your recognition engine. Choose collaborators who represent what you want to be known for, and support others who do the same.

Takeaway: Community multiplies your reputation. The people beside you shape how the world sees you.

COMPETENCE

Competence is about doing the thing properly; having the skill, reliability, and discipline to deliver what you promise.

Good intentions don't build trust on their own. You can be the nicest person on Earth, but if you can't follow through, people stop believing. Competence shows up through great execution, clear processes, and consistent delivery. When clients can see that you take your craft seriously, they relax.

For designers, competence is often your loudest signal. Every interaction, from your work to your emails, adds another layer of trust.

Takeaway: Competence is confidence, proven through reliable action.

NARRATIVE

Narrative is the story people tell about you, and the story you tell about yourself. It lives in the space between perception and truth.

Every reputation lives inside a story. If you don't guide it, others will, and their version might not match the reality. A strong narrative makes what you do meaningful and memorable. It shows up through your visuals, words, and actions—all the touchpoints where people experience your brand.

As designers, our job is to help brands tell that truth clearly and consistently. Every colour, font, and phrase should reinforce the same story.

Takeaway: Narrative is how your reputation speaks when you're not in the room.

You've probably noticed how important evidence is now, and each part of the grid depends on it. People don't trust what you do once; they trust what you keep doing. Anyone can act with integrity once or tell a great story once, but what people trust are the patterns. They trust that you keep showing up, keep delivering, keep proving the story true.

When integrity, competence, community, and narrative work together, backed by real evidence and repeated with consistency, reputation turns into an unforgettable brand. That's when trust compounds.

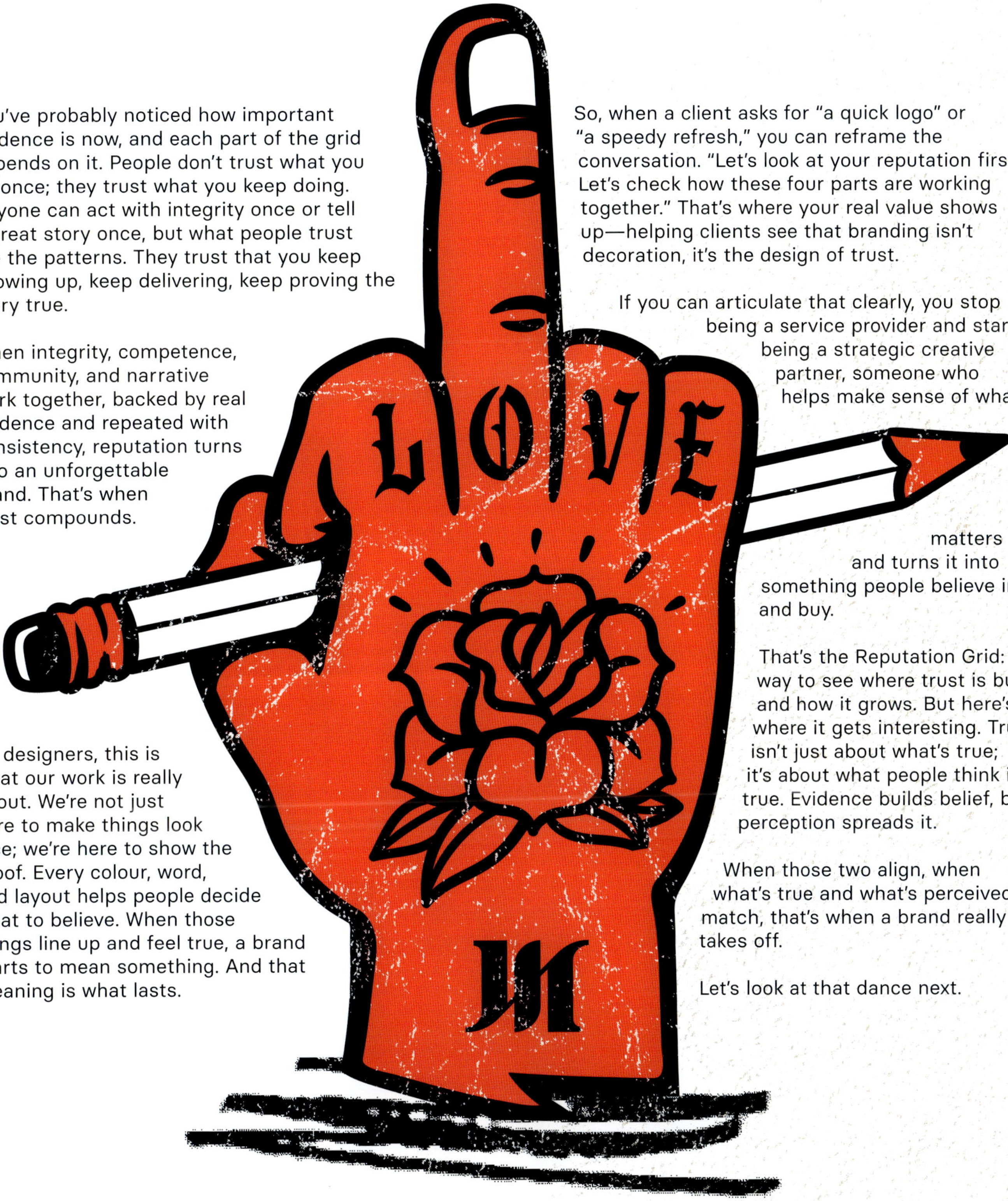

As designers, this is what our work is really about. We're not just here to make things look nice; we're here to show the proof. Every colour, word, and layout helps people decide what to believe. When those things line up and feel true, a brand starts to mean something. And that meaning is what lasts.

So, when a client asks for "a quick logo" or "a speedy refresh," you can reframe the conversation. "Let's look at your reputation first. Let's check how these four parts are working together." That's where your real value shows up—helping clients see that branding isn't decoration, it's the design of trust.

If you can articulate that clearly, you stop being a service provider and start being a strategic creative partner, someone who helps make sense of what matters and turns it into something people believe in and buy.

That's the Reputation Grid: a way to see where trust is built and how it grows. But here's where it gets interesting. Trust isn't just about what's true; it's about what people think is true. Evidence builds belief, but perception spreads it.

When those two align, when what's true and what's perceived match, that's when a brand really takes off.

Let's look at that dance next.

PERCEPTION VS. EVIDENCE

At the heart of every brand are two forces at play: **perception** and **evidence**.

Evidence is what *you've actually done*. It's the real, tangible proof of your work. The products you've built, the testimonials you've earned, the projects you've delivered, the impact you've created. It's the truth, the receipts, the stuff that stands up in a court of law.

Perception, on the other hand, is what *people think you've done*. It's how your brand is experienced from the outside. It's the story that forms in someone's head before they ever meet you, talk to you, or buy from you.

The fact of the matter is, not everyone has access to all the evidence.

Most people won't see the hours you've poured in, the thinking behind it, or how much effort goes into what you do. They just see the end result, like the logo, the illustration, or the way you show up, and that's where their opinion forms. People make their minds up based on what they can see, not what's actually true.

That's why perception, in many cases, outweighs evidence. You could be absolutely brilliant at what you do, but if nobody knows it, it doesn't exist in their world. You might have the work to back it up, but if the way you show up looks sloppy or inconsistent, people will think twice.

That doesn't mean perception is about pretending or faking it. It's about making it easier for people to see what's real. The closer you can bring what's true and what's seen together, the stronger your brand becomes. Your job as a brand builder is to make sure the outside world's perception matches the inside truth . . . or at least gets as close as possible.

Trust doesn't come from either perception or evidence on its own. It grows when the two work together, as you can see from the diagram (opposite) and description below.

> **High evidence, high perception:**
> The Power Brand. This is where trust, reputation, and longevity live.
>
> **Low evidence, high perception:**
> The Hype Brand. Looks great from the outside, but burns fast and fades faster.
>
> **High evidence, low perception:**
> The Hidden Genius Brand. You're doing great work, but nobody knows about it.
>
> **Low evidence, low perception:**
> The Work-in-Progress Brand. You've got work to do, but everyone starts here.

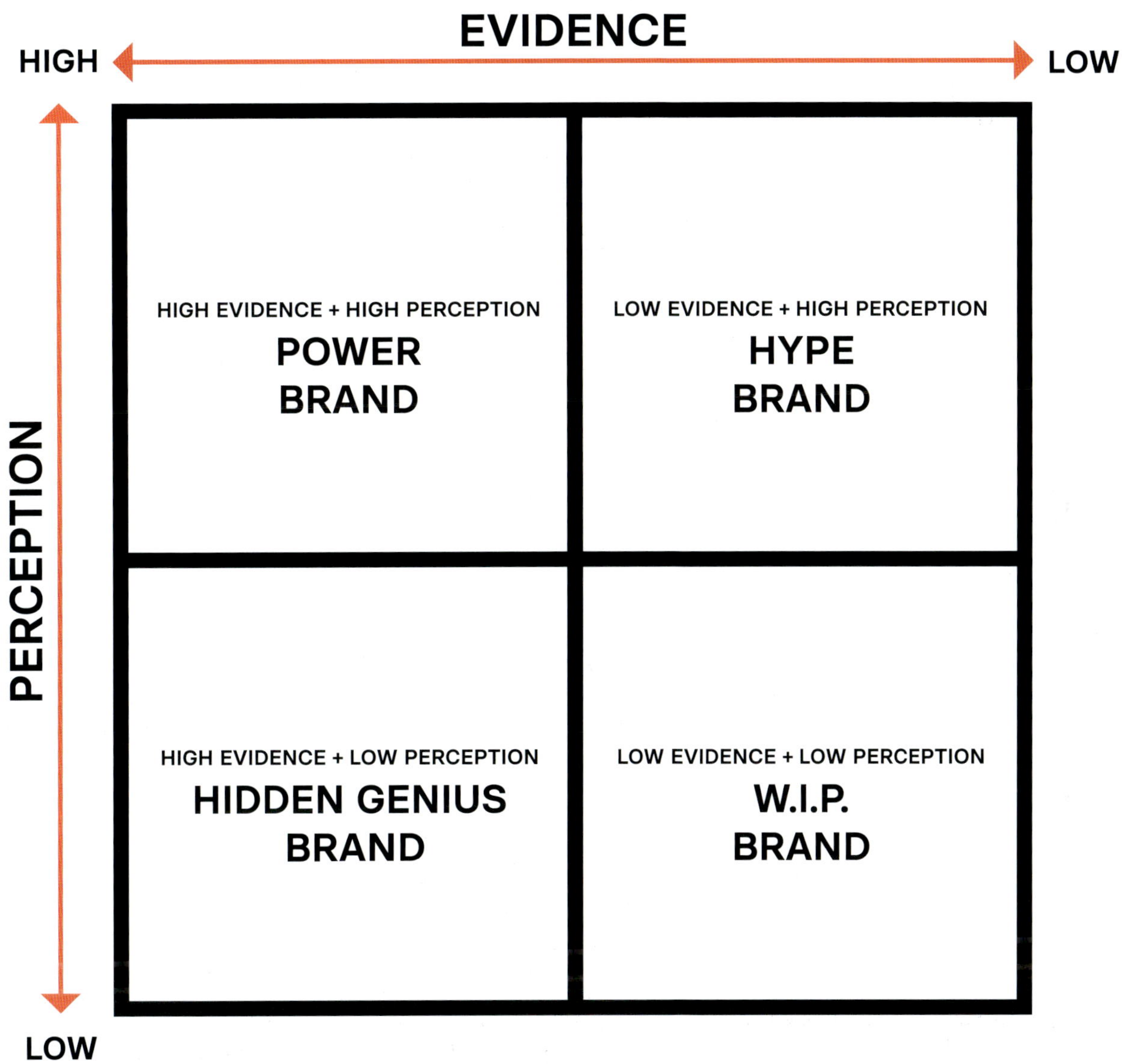

If you think about it, every great brand masters the balance between perception and evidence. Apple didn't just make great products . . . they built a perception of innovation, precision, and taste. Nike doesn't just make trainers . . . they've created a perception of movement, attitude, and belief. The evidence backs it all up, but it's perception that draws people in first.

That's why your reputation isn't just what you've done, it's what people *think* you've done.

At the end of the day, branding isn't just about reality. It's about *perceived* reality.

Lincoln 10 Year Artwork

Lincoln limited edition whiskey

Chapter Ten -

BEHIND THE CURTAIN: THE DDD PROCESS

When I first started out in design, I pretty much did everything wrong. And I don't just mean a couple of silly mistakes here and there. I mean everything you could possibly get wrong, I managed to do wrong. Looking back now, it's almost funny . . . almost.

I had no clue what I was doing. No structure meant no process, and without a process, I had zero clarity on what my clients actually wanted. Most of the time I was just winging it and hoping for the best. I was the guy who said yes to unlimited revisions, which, if you've ever done it, you'll know is basically digging your own grave. I never set timelines, so projects dragged on forever. And because I didn't ask the right questions, I spent most of the time guessing myself into creative anxiety.

On some projects, I handed over too much control; others, I shut people out completely. I just couldn't find the balance.

There's one project that's burned into my brain. I won't name the client, but let's just say they took full advantage of my "unlimited revisions" promise. And when I said "unlimited," I meant it. I kept going until they were happy, because I thought that was my job. The problem was, without any clarity to guide us, we never got there. I ended up producing over eighty variations of a single logo and we never agreed on a direction. I refunded the project and called it a day. We both lost.

That was the pattern in my early years: a cycle of chaos that kept repeating. And chaos is expensive. It eats your time, your money, and your headspace. After years of messing things up and learning the hard way, I finally realised the truth:

PROCESS ISN'T A PRISON. IT'S FREEDOM.

A good process doesn't box you in; it gives you a foundation to build from. It evolves with you. It gives your creativity room to breathe, keeps things moving, and stops you from losing your mind halfway through.

Before we get into it, I want to be clear: What I'm about to share is my process. The way my studio works, the way my team and I bring ideas to life with our clients. Other designers will have their own way, and that's the point. There's no single right way to build a brand. There are hundreds of paths to a great result, and this just happens to be mine.

The DDD process—Discover, Design, Deliver—is how I keep projects structured, intentional, and actually enjoyable.

Where it came from

I didn't invent DDD overnight. It started as a simple way to explain what I was already doing, but in language that made sense to clients. Most people came to me asking for a logo, not a brand. I needed a way to show that good design isn't just about making something look nice; it's about following a process that makes it work.

So I started saying, "First we do Discovery, then Design, then Delivery." You can't really jump the queue, because each stage sets up the next. Once I began explaining it that way, everything clicked. Projects ran smoother, clients understood why we did what we did, and the work got stronger.

Now, this is a simplified version of what really happens in my studio. Every project is different, but it shows the shape of things. Think of this as the everyday version, a practical look at how a brand actually comes together.

1 DISCOVER

Every idea starts here. Discovery is where we slow things down and take the time to understand what we're building. It's about asking the right questions, digging into the story behind the work, and shaping the foundation before design even begins.

When everyone's aligned, the whole project flows better. The direction feels clear, people feel confident, and energy builds around what's coming next.

In my studio, this usually starts with a ninety-minute call. We chat about their business, audience, and goals. I use a framework called the Five Idea Keys to make sure we cover everything that matters (you'll see more on that later). After the session, we summarise everything into a simple PDF that acts as a mini brief. It gets signed off before design starts, so everyone knows what we're building and why. That clarity saves weeks of confusion later.

Takeaway: Discovery builds clarity. And clarity saves you from chaos.

2 DESIGN

Design is where ideas start to take shape. Everything that was just talk now becomes something you can see and feel. It's problem solving with creativity.

We use what we learned in Discovery to make decisions that are grounded in strategy. Every logo, colour, and type choice has a reason behind it. When clients see that logic, they stop guessing and start trusting.

In my studio, we sketch, explore, and share early ideas quickly. We get feedback before refining too far, so we don't waste time polishing the wrong thing. The goal isn't endless versions, it's alignment. Once we've got a direction, we develop it into a complete identity that can grow and evolve with the brand.

Takeaway: Design turns clarity into form. It's where trust starts to take shape.

3 DELIVER

Delivery is where everything you've built gets ready for the real world. It's not just sending final files; it's helping clients use what you've made with confidence.

Before we deliver, we check what they'll actually need. There's no point giving someone 400 templates they'll never touch. We give them the tools that make their brand usable and practical: logo files, colours, typefaces, and a simple set of guidelines. Nothing bloated, just what they need to stay consistent.

We also walk them through everything. We don't just send and vanish. We make sure they understand how to use what we've created so it doesn't gather dust in a folder. When clients feel supported, they come back. That's how reputations are built.

Takeaway: Delivery isn't the end. It's the start of the brand's real life.

BRINGING IT ALL TOGETHER

The DDD process has become one of my most valuable tools—not just for running projects, but for explaining what I do. When you can clearly show how things work, clients understand your value instantly. It builds trust, shows confidence, and makes winning work so much easier. A simple, easy-to-explain process isn't just good design practice, it's one of the best sales tools you'll ever have.

Now that you've seen how I do it, let's mix things up. In the next chapter, I'll introduce you to a few friends from around the world who each do things their own way. They've got stories, lessons, and plenty of wisdom to share. So grab a drink, get comfy, and let's see what we can learn from some of the best in the game.

DDD PROCESS

ALRIGHT!
TEAM

Chapter Eleven -

WISDOM FROM THE BEST — A ROUNDTABLE CHIN-WAG

I've always believed that the environment you build around yourself as a designer makes all the difference. The people you spend time with, the ones you bounce ideas off, the ones who keep you thinking; they all shape how you grow.

Some of the biggest lessons I've ever learned haven't come from books or courses; they've come from conversations. Sitting with other designers, swapping stories, hearing how they do things. Every chat gives you a new way to look at your own work and pushes you to see things differently.

So, for this chapter, in addition to showing some of their work, I wanted to bring a few of those voices to you. Three friends, three studios, three different parts of the world. I asked them four simple questions:

1. What's your best branding advice for someone starting out with no money?

2. What hasn't changed in the industry since you started out?

3. What's one question more clients should be asking?

4. What's a piece of "industry wisdom" you actually disagree with?

So . . . pull up a chair and get comfy. The drinks are on me.

1. WHAT'S YOUR BEST BRANDING ADVICE FOR SOMEONE STARTING OUT WITH NO MONEY?

HEY STUDIO /// Verònica Fuerte:
If you don't have money, keep your expectations realistic. Use what's available to you. If you have a friend who knows design, ask for help. If you can do a little yourself, make something simple and clear. At the beginning, you just need something that works. Don't obsess about being unique or perfect. Even taking inspiration from something you like is fine. Later, when you can afford it, you'll invest in proper branding. Just remember, if you want to grow, that investment will be necessary.

LINCOLN DESIGN CO. /// Dan Janssen:
Don't obsess over your logo yet—start with your network. Who actually knows about your idea? Who are you talking to? You can't build a brand in isolation. Networking is free, and it's often worth more than design in the early days. Show up, have conversations, connect with people online and in person. Every connection you make could be your first customer, biggest supporter, or someone who introduces you to the right opportunity. A strong network will carry your brand way further than a fancy design ever will.

PENNYBRIDGE /// Paul Balfe:
Start with clarity, not polish. Figure out what you stand for, why you exist, and who you're talking to. If you can explain that in a single sentence and stay consistent with it, you've already got the foundation of a brand. Everything else like the logo, colours, and campaigns can come later. Spend your early energy understanding yourself, not decorating yourself.

2. WHAT HASN'T CHANGED IN THE INDUSTRY SINCE YOU STARTED OUT?

HEY STUDIO /// Verònica Fuerte:
When I started more than twenty years ago, we could spend six months on an identity. Now it's three weeks, sometimes less. The pressure of time has completely flipped. Everything is faster. But what hasn't changed is the essence: You still need a strong idea, you still need craft, and you still need clarity. Tools and timing evolve, but those foundations stay the same.

LINCOLN DESIGN CO. /// Dan Janssen:
You can't fake passion. Whether you're building a brand, a product, or a service—you have to love it enough to go all in. That energy seeps into everything you do. And here's the truth: Skill is learnable, but taste isn't. Just because you can make something doesn't mean it will connect. Developing your eye, knowing what feels right, what looks good, what resonates—that takes years of paying attention and practicing. Don't shortcut that process.

PENNYBRIDGE /// Paul Balfe:
The power of story. Tools change and trends come and go, but people still connect with stories they can see themselves in. No amount of tech or tactics will ever replace that human connection. It's always been about meaning and helping people feel something real.

3. WHAT'S ONE QUESTION MORE CLIENTS SHOULD BE ASKING?

HEY STUDIO /// Verònica Fuerte:
I wish more clients said: ***"I trust you—what do you think is best?"*** Like when you go to the doctor, you don't tell them how to treat you . . . you trust their expertise. Design often gets confused with personal taste: *"I like this colour. I don't like that font."* But that's not the point. Clients hire us for our vision and experience. Sometimes the best thing they can say is simply: You choose.

LINCOLN DESIGN CO. /// Dan Janssen:
If you're working with a creative, the best thing you can ask is: ***"What do you need from me to make this smoother?"*** It sounds simple, but communication is everything. Designers aren't mind readers. When you give clear, timely feedback, even if it's just a quick note that you've received the work, it builds respect and momentum. Silence kills projects faster than anything else. Brands are built in partnership, and that partnership starts with clear communication.

PENNYBRIDGE /// Paul Balfe:
"How do we make people care?" Not *"How do we sell more stuff by Friday?"* If you can make people care, the rest follows. It's easy to focus on quick returns, but lasting brands are built on emotional connection, not short-term wins.

4. WHAT'S A PIECE OF "INDUSTRY WISDOM" YOU ACTUALLY DISAGREE WITH?

HEY STUDIO /// Verònica Fuerte:
That you always need a "brand strategist" before design can happen. I respect the role, but honestly, designers can ask the right questions and shape strategy through the work itself. All the "What's your why, who's your audience, what's your purpose" frameworks are fine, but they're not magic. Sometimes they only slow things down. I believe design can lead strategy, not just decorate it.

LINCOLN DESIGN CO. /// Dan Janssen:
Some people will tell you that you should only ever see one logo option from a designer. I think that's rubbish. Branding is a collaborative process, not a big reveal. You should see the journey, the thinking, the directions explored, because that's how you build something together that lasts.

PENNYBRIDGE /// Paul Balfe:
Brand guidelines and brands being "finished." They're never finished. A brand isn't a logo, a deck, or a set of rules. It's a living thing that evolves every single day. The guidelines and presentations might help you start, but the real brand is built in the everyday moments. How you show up, how you treat people, how you make them feel. That's what makes people fall in love with certain brands over others.

LINCOLN DESIGN CO.

Lincoln Design Co. is a full-service brand design agency specializing in sports, lifestyle, outdoor, and entertainment industries. Working closely with world-class brands like Hot Wheels, Tony Hawk, Nike, Universal Pictures, Monster Energy and Hasbro to bring to market visual solutions to elevate their brands.

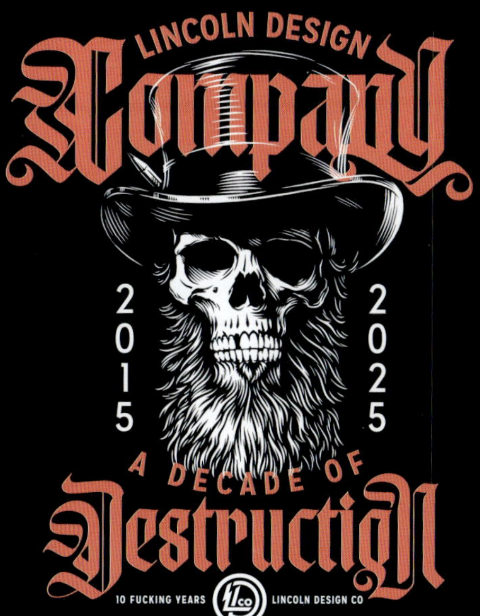

Lincoln DESIGN
LINCOLN DESIGN CO
LINCOLN DESIGN CO
LINCOLN DESIGN
LINCOLN DESIGN CO USA
LINCOLN
HONEST
LINCOLN
Lincoln DESIGN

FORTNITE
GRRIZ
YOU DROPPED THIS CROWN

FORTNITE
LLAMA HERE!
DEFY THE STORM
VICTORY ROYALE
PROPERTY OF TILTED TOWERS

FORTNITE
LOOTDROP SUMMER 2022
AGE IT UP
MORE STYLE
BE ICONIC
DEFY THE STORM
MEOW
LYNX

nickelodeon
TOTAL TURTLE POWER
RISE OF THE TEENAGE MUTANT NINJA TURTLES

TOTAL TURTLE POWER

NERF PRO
GEL FIRE

NERF PRO
GEL FIRE

SCENARIO
LANDO
SEVEN
NORRIS
RACING
4
LNY
Lando Norris
LANDO
NORRIS
Lando
4
L4NDo

ELITE
COLLECTION
TOUGH
TALKERS
BEND 'N' BASH
DECADE OF
DOMINATION
LIVE
ACTION
BATTLE
PACK
BECOME A
SUPERSTAR
COMBO
CRUSHERS
WRESTLEMANIA
MAIN EVENT
SERIES
HOLLYWOOD
SOUND
SLAMMERS
MR.T
SURVIVOR
SERIES

STING
CHAMPIONSHIP
SHOWDOWN
AUSTIN THEORY
VS
DEFINING
MOMENTS

HEY STUDIO
Hey is a Barcelona-based creative studio founded in 2007. They specialize in developing creative strategies and visual languages for clients around the world. Their collaborative approach and passionate team enable them to create impactful designs that meet client needs and resonate with target audiences.

Hey Hola Coffee
Guatemala
250g

Caravelle
Soda
Lemon & Ginger
Organically Sweetened
Hibiscus & Pomelo
Organically Sweetened
Cherry Lemonade
Organically Sweetened

Caravelle
spritz
vermut
bloody mary
elderflower sangria
random concoction

Soda
Lemon & Ginger
Hibiscus & Pomelo
Cherry Lemonade
Orange & Passionfruit
Soda Reimagined
Crafted in Barcelona
@caravellesoda
caravellebrewery.com
Orange
Soda
Lemon
Caravelle

origo

casa ñidro
644693097
@casa_nidro
casanidro.com

casa ñidro

Hey
Women at Work
Hey

Hey
Hey

EXTINTOR
Hey

arrels

FEET ON THE GROUND, HEAD IN THE CLOUDS

10 blocks
6 puzzles

Caravelle
Caravelle
Caravelle
Caravelle

PENNYBRIDGE

PENNYBRIDGE CREATIVE

Pennybridge is an unconventionally professional creative studio based in Palm Beach on the sunny Gold Coast, Australia. With an eclectic range of disciplines, from illustration and brand design to large-scale murals and web design, the solid team at Pennybridge believes in the power of creative partnerships, playful collaboration and damn good design!

PENNYBRIDGE

SOCIAL
Social Espresso, bringing people together

EARTH
HIGH COUNTRY

PENNYBRIDGE
PALM GARDEN
AN UNCONVENTIONALLY
PROFESSIONAL
CREATIVE STUDIO™

LAZY ALE
PENNYBRIDGE CREATIVE
TURNING CHAOS TO CLARITY

FROM THE HEART
TOGETHER WE RISE

EXTRAORDINARY
AWAITS
THE PINK HOTEL
TEQUILA HERRADURA
COOLANGATTA

19TH AVE
PENNYBRIDGE
PENNYBRIDGE
PENNYBRIDGE

Innovative solutions made real through expert 3D printing.
PRECISION AT EVERY LAYER
Transforming concepts into tangible creations with advanced 3D printing.
FORMA
Forma 3D

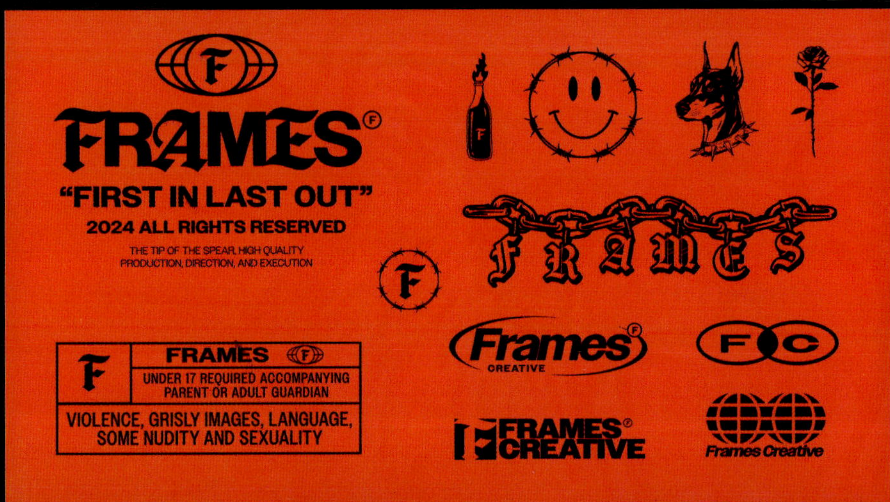

An *unconventionally* professional *creative* studio

STAND OUT
DON'T BLEND IN

Chapter Twelve -

SIMPLE CASE STUDIES - DDD STYLE

In this section, I want to show you how the DDD process actually plays out in real life. We're going to look at five very different client projects: Wilden, Ridgefield, Craft Accords, The Happy Toolbox, and Team 13. Each one had its own story, its own challenges, and its own way of coming to life. That's the fun part of this job, because no two brands are ever the same.

For each project, I'll walk you through what we discovered, how we made the design decisions, and what we delivered at the end. It's a simple way to show how the process works, step by step, without any added fluff . . . you have read a lot of words so far, so I want your eyes to have a bit of fun.

I think it's important to actually see this process in action because it proves that clarity and structure don't kill creativity; they give it direction. So let's dive in and take a look at how raw ideas turned into real brands.

WILDEN

The fresh, fast, and fun approach to landscape design

DISCOVER

Wilden came to us with a bold idea. They wanted to make professional landscape architecture accessible through a simple online service. The mission was bigger than just gardens, though . . . it was really about helping people reconnect with nature, starting right at home.

They didn't want to be seen as just another garden company. They wanted to grow the business, attract new homeowners, and appeal to a younger, eco-minded audience. During our first discovery call, one of the things that came up straight away was how tricky people found the name to pronounce. Some said "Wild N," others "Will Den," and it quickly became clear that this confusion was holding them back. So, when we moved into the design phase, we already knew this was one of the first problems we'd need to think about.

DESIGN

We solved the pronunciation problem inside the logo. The sideways "E" also reads as a "W" when flipped, which helped people instantly understand how to say the name and gave the brand a neat little visual twist to remember it by. From there, everything started to fall into place.

The colour palette mixed minty greens and soft lilacs to keep things fresh, modern, and connected to nature without drifting into the usual eco clichés. We brought in hand-drawn illustrations and friendly layouts to make it feel human and easy to connect with.

To build out the wider visual identity, I spent time gathering Will's original notes and sketches from the gardens he designed. The way he highlighted, circled, and marked ideas on the fly had its own creative rhythm, so I used that style as the foundation for the visual language. It created a natural consistency between how he works and how the brand looks, making the whole thing feel unmistakably "Wilden."

The end result felt wild at heart, but still calm and considered—a brand that had energy, but knew where it was going.

DELIVER

Delivery for Wilden was all about setting them up to use the brand with confidence. We focused on building simple, flexible templates that made it easy for them to stay consistent without needing a designer every time to execute. By using the bird's-eye-view shapes from garden layouts, we were able to house different bits of information like headers and titles, and use some of the illustrative icons as visual nods to garden design. Those same elements became a clever way to build out the wider visual identity.

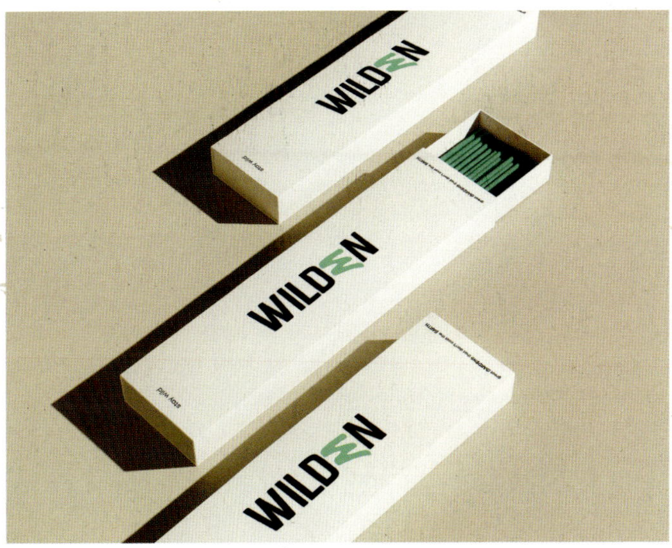

RIDGEFIELD PLAYHOUSE

Big acts. Small-town magic.

DISCOVER

Ridgefield Playhouse came to us with a clear goal: to evolve their identity and position themselves as more than just a venue. They were already loved locally, hosting incredible talent and community events, but wanted to be seen as a cultural destination in their own right.

Through discovery, we realised the playhouse was as much about connection as performance. People came for the experience, not just the big names. They wanted a brand that could speak to loyal patrons while also welcoming a younger audience: people in their thirties and forties looking for world-class entertainment without leaving town.

The team was doing brilliant work, but the brand had not kept pace. It felt dated and disconnected. We worked with them to clarify what made Ridgefield special: a nonprofit that reinvests in arts and education while bringing global talent to a local stage. The goal was to give them a brand they could stand behind proudly, one that reflected the magic happening inside those walls.

DESIGN

This identity needed to work hard. Ridgefield runs concerts, community programs, and education initiatives, so the brand had to be flexible and easy to apply across everything they do.

We built the system around big, confident typography and a bold R mark that captured the playhouse's rhythm and warmth. Hidden inside the letter is a musical note, a subtle nod to performance, creativity, and the energy that fills the space.

The colour palette reflected the variety of what happens inside. We created combinations of warm neutrals and vivid tones so each poster or event could have its own character while still feeling part of the same family. The result was a visual system that felt expressive and human, giving Ridgefield a clear, modern identity that could grow and evolve with them.

DELIVER

For delivery, we focused less on designing every touchpoint and more on building a framework the Ridgefield team could grow from. With their twenty-fifth anniversary approaching, this was the moment to reconnect.

We created a flexible system that gave their in-house team direction and freedom, helping them translate the brand across everything from event posters to digital campaigns. The layouts we explored became a guide for future design decisions, giving the team confidence and clarity.

We also introduced a sub-brand framework for their community and education programs, giving each initiative its own identity within the wider Ridgefield family. The result was a tool kit full of life, personality, and room to grow—something that brought the playhouse back into alignment with its mission to champion creativity, welcome new audiences, and celebrate culture in all its forms.

RIDGEFIELD
PLAYHOUSE

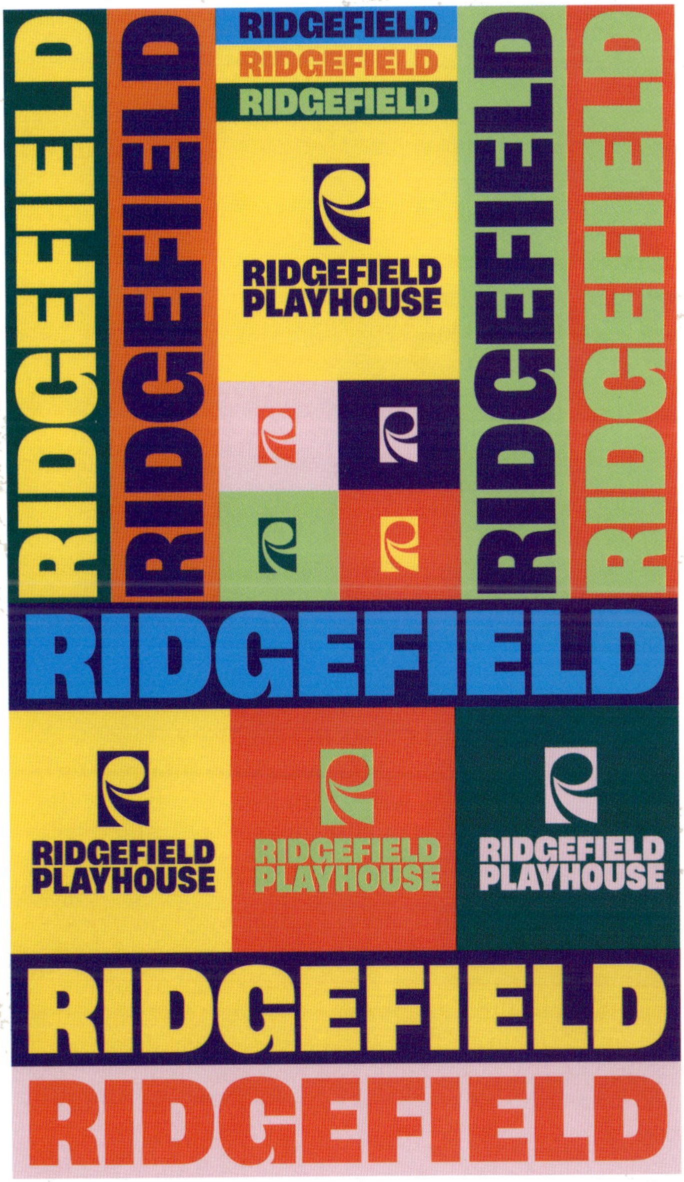
RIDGEFIELD
RIDGEFIELD
RIDGEFIELD
RIDGEFIELD
RIDGEFIELD
RIDGEFIELD PLAYHOUSE
RIDGEFIELD
RIDGEFIELD
RIDGEFIELD
RIDGEFIELD PLAYHOUSE
RIDGEFIELD PLAYHOUSE
RIDGEFIELD PLAYHOUSE
RIDGEFIELD
RIDGEFIELD

SOLD OUT
SOLD OUT
SOLD OUT
APRIL 9TH 2025
SAMARA JOY

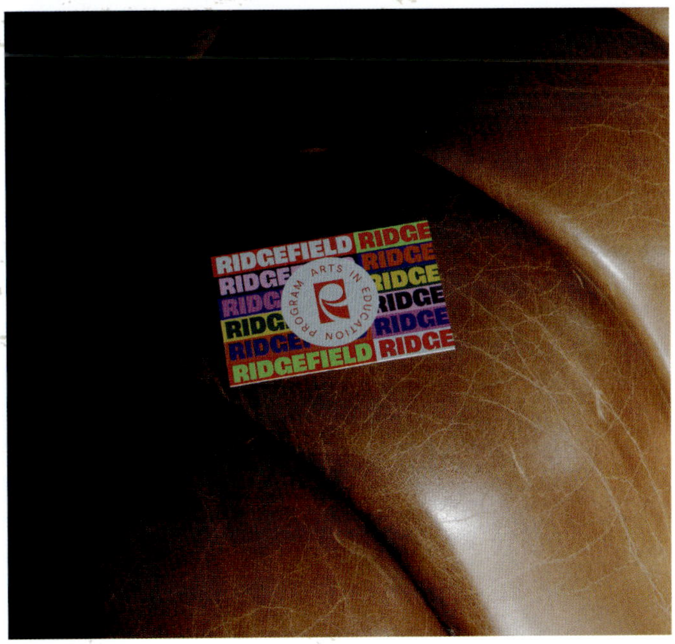
RIDGEFIELD
PROGRAM ARTS IN EDUCATION
RIDGEFIELD

CRAFT ACCORDS

Where curiosity becomes craft, turning everyday drinks into sensory experiences

DISCOVER

Craft Accords (CA) started out as a small coffee cart in Hermosa Beach, but Stefan's idea was much bigger than serving coffee. He wanted to change the way people think about nonalcoholic drinks, treating coffee, tea, and refreshment with the same care and creativity as a cocktail. The big challenge was how to stand out in a world full of cafés that all look and sound the same.

When we talked things through, we realised the real story wasn't about drinks at all. It was about curiosity. Craft Accords was creating little moments that made people stop, taste, and smile. Every drink was designed as a small sensory experience. Their audience wasn't just coffee lovers, they were curious people who loved design, culture, and the discovery of new things.

DESIGN

We wanted the design to feel as curious and layered as the drinks themselves. We played with the idea of opposites coming together, things that shouldn't work, but somehow do. That thinking led to the chosen concept . . . a wolf riding a tricycle with a daisy for a head. It sounded wild, but it captured the heart of the brand perfectly. It was playful, unexpected, and full of character.

Around that we built a visual system that could flex. It could be bold and loud one moment and calm and thoughtful the next. The "Curious Collective" tagline set the tone, and the alternate CA monogram became a simple little mark that worked beautifully across packaging and merch. We tucked it into small places like the bottom of cups so the people who were curious, and looked for randomness, got a visual reward.

DELIVER

The goal was to give Stefan a brand he could actually use straight away. We focused on the practical things first: cups, menus, signage, packaging, loyalty cards, all the bits he needed to show up consistently from day one.

We also thought about how the brand could grow over time. By pulling the daisy out of the main logo, we created a standalone shape that worked for patterns and merch. It became a usable element we could flex across tote bags, takeaway bags, and other products. When someone grabs a drink from Craft Accords, they're not just getting coffee—they're getting a little moment of joy to take with them.

HAPPY
TOOLBOX

HAPPY
TOOLBOX

THE HAPPY TOOLBOX

Where fun meets function

DISCOVER

The Happy Toolbox was already an established name when they came to us. They didn't need a full rebrand; they just wanted to refresh things a little. The goal was to sharpen up the visual identity so everything felt more cohesive and usable across their website, packaging, and marketing. From the start, it was obvious that this brand was all about having fun and not taking itself too seriously. Their 3D models already had this playful, characterful energy to them, and we wanted to bring that same spirit into the design system.

We knew the brand needed to keep its sense of humour while still looking clean and confident enough to attract professional creators, agencies, and developers. It was about finding the sweet spot between fun and functional.

DESIGN

When it came to design, we wanted to keep the brand feeling lighthearted and approachable while holding on to its joyful energy. The original identity already had strong foundations, so this was more about refining what was there and giving it new life. The main goal was to give The Happy Toolbox team freedom, the ability to have fun, be playful, and express themselves through the brand.

We created a mascot that could be as fun or as silly as they wanted it to be. The toolbox character became their playground, a place where personality could really shine. It gave them a visual anchor they could build on and adapt for different moments. For example, when they were out of office, they could use a little version of the character to show it in a playful way.

The palette of bold oranges, clean blues, and soft off-whites brought a cheerful energy that still felt balanced and professional. Typography tied it all together with a mix of friendly display type for headlines and clean, legible fonts for everything else.

DELIVER

The delivery focused on building a tool kit the team could use with ease every day. We created clear brand guidelines that showed how to apply the logo, type, and colours consistently across all online spaces. Because most of The Happy Toolbox lives and operates online, we focused on delivering digital files and assets they could use across their website, platform, and social channels.

We also had some fun exploring a few physical pieces. The team loved the character so much that we created patterns and merch they could wear and use in the studio. It was a small touch, but it gave the brand an extra sense of personality and pride . . . I think there might even be a plushy somewhere in the world.

TEAM 13

Leave the drama on the screen

DISCOVER

Team 13 already had a great reputation and were working with some fantastic clients, but as the company grew, they started to lose sight of who they were as a brand. The business had expanded quickly and naturally, but the brand hadn't kept pace.

We spent time helping them define who they were, what they stood for, and how they wanted to show up. They were brilliant at telling other people's stories, but found it hard to tell their own, so that became our focus.

We stripped everything back to a few simple truths. *We make videos. Leave the drama on the screen. When it snows, we go skiing.* Those lines summed them up perfectly—straightforward, good-humoured, and confident. It gave them a voice that finally sounded like them and set the foundation for everything that followed.

DESIGN

The design direction came from Matt's story. The name was born from his teenage ski crew, a group of friends who filmed each other on the slopes and called themselves Team 13. That sense of friendship and adventure became the heartbeat of the brand.

We channelled that energy through a colour palette inspired by retro ski suits from the early 80s—bright, nostalgic, and full of life. Matt's love of old horror and indie films sparked a hand-drawn, slightly imperfect

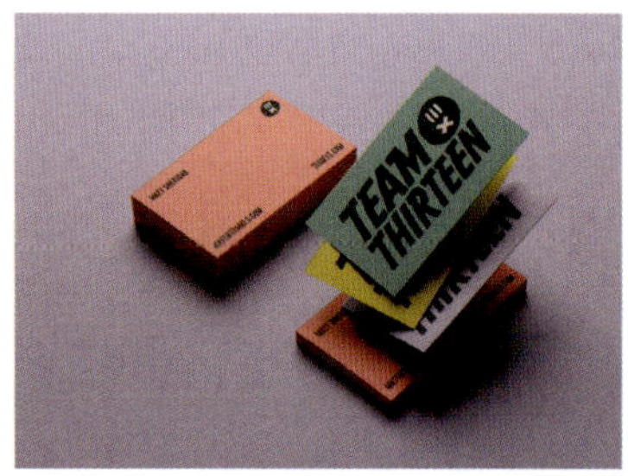

type style that gave the brand its edge. It felt creative, confident, and a little rebellious.

We then built a simple icon system to tie it all together. The XIII lockup (13 in Roman numerals) became the mascot. The three lines formed eyes, the X a mouth, creating a subtle face that hinted at their personality. It also carried a deeper meaning. During discovery, we learned they often found it hard to talk about themselves, so the X over the mouth became a quiet, clever nod to that truth.

DELIVER

Delivery was all about making it easy for the Team 13 crew to bring their brand to life. Because their world revolves around motion, we focused on animation-ready assets, title cards, and graphics that could move and adapt.

We also created a full set of presentation and pitch decks they could customise for client work, helping them communicate clearly and consistently. Alongside this, we produced all the brand assets they'd need to roll things out further—everything built with flexibility in mind so the identity could grow naturally and find its way onto merch, stickers, and gear in the future.

MBJ
HOTEL
Welcome

Chapter Thirteen -

THE THINGS THAT NEVER CHANGE IN BRANDING

There's this hotel in London called The Treehouse. It's a place that Kate and I stayed in a lot while we were going through our in-vitro fertilisation (IVF) journey, trying to have a baby. We'd been through quite a bit by that point . . . a few miscarriages and a lot of heartbreak. IVF was our only real chance, and anyone who's been through that or knows someone who has will understand how tough it can be. (And if that's you, or someone close to you, I see you.)

Every time we had to go up to London for treatment, we stayed there. It became our little home away from home for a couple of years. The people at The Treehouse were just different. They were kind, thoughtful, and always went out of their way to make things easy for us. They greeted us with real smiles, remembered our names, and made everything feel effortless.

By now, you'll know that Rocco is here. He's that wild little one I mentioned in the intro, the kid who eats food off the floor and keeps us on our toes. We went back to London not long after he was born to see some friends, and of course we stayed at The Treehouse again.

When we did the online check-in, we'd mentioned there were three of us this time, and they'd clearly noticed. When we got up to the room, there was a little Paddington Bear toy sitting on the bed with a handwritten note welcoming us all back. It wasn't over the top, just simple and thoughtful, and it's something I've never forgotten. It's also something I now tell everyone about.

That moment made me start thinking about my own work differently, not just the design itself, but the experience people have when they work with me.

Since then, we've always gone back to that hotel. And whenever friends ask where to stay in London, that's the first place we recommend. It wasn't just one small act of care; it was that small act built on top of a consistently great experience every time we stayed there that turned us into loyal fans and advocates. That, to me, is what branding is really about. It's not just what you do, it's how you make people feel.

For me, that's the thing that never changes in branding. The brands that focus on creating great experiences are the ones people remember and talk about.

I've developed a bit of an obsession with hospitality. I honestly think we can all learn a lot from it. As creatives, we spend so much time looking at what other designers are doing when sometimes the best lessons come from completely different worlds. There's so much we can borrow from the way great hotels, restaurants, or even coffee shops make people feel cared for. So, I started paying attention to that and thinking about how I could bring some of that hospitality mindset into my own work. I asked myself: "What if I looked after my clients like a boutique hotel looks after their guests?"

Now, I'm definitely not perfect at it, but over the years I've found a few things that are easy to do and make a real difference. Think of them as small ways to add a bit more warmth and jazz to your projects. Here are a few you can try yourself.

1. Surprise and Delight

This is all about small, thoughtful gestures that go a long way. Think of it as the design version of chocolates on the pillow. When you're on a discovery call, ask your client a few genuine questions about their life. ***What did you do at the weekend? Are you reading anything interesting right now?*** Little details like that can give you clues for a small, personal gift later on. And if nothing comes to mind, send them a few of your sketches they can stick up on the wall in their office. It's simple, but it makes people smile and shows that you care.

2. The Ikos Impression

This one's all about the onboarding process. Kate and I once stayed at the Ikos resort in Greece, and their welcoming sequence was absolutely spot-on. We were picked up from the airport in a spotless car, driven by a friendly guy who chatted the whole way. When we arrived, the staff handled our bags, handed us drinks and cold towels, and made the whole thing feel effortless. It was perfect. And the best part? You could tell it wasn't a one-off. They were doing it for every guest who walked through the door.

That's the halo effect in action. A great first impression makes you instantly confident that the rest of the experience is going to be just as good. The same applies to us as designers. When a client first signs on, that early experience sets the tone for everything that follows. Get your onboarding right, and they'll trust that the rest of the process will be just as smooth.

3. The Handover Cuddle

Set your clients up for success. Once you've delivered everything, don't just send the files and vanish. Put together a simple ninety-day plan that outlines what comes next. It could include things like updating their website, rolling out new assets on social media, or planning a small launch day to show off the new brand.

This plan can be a little gift you hand over at the end of the project. It shows you care about what happens after the work goes live, and it also positions you perfectly to help with the next stage. It's an easy way to keep momentum going, build trust, and turn one project into an ongoing relationship.

Now, I'm not saying you need to do all of these things for every client. You don't need to go over the top or spend loads of money. But adding an extra thirty dollars to your quote can give you a bit of room to do something thoughtful. Maybe it's sending a book, a handwritten note, or a quick sketch during the middle of the project to boost the client's energy. Small things like that go a long way. They show you actually care, and they stick in people's minds long after the work is done. They're good reputation builders.

It's much easier to keep a client than it is to find a new one, so making the experience of working with you fun, memorable, and consistent will do more for your brand's growth than any marketing campaign ever could. When people enjoy the process, they come back and they talk about you to all their friends.

And that's where this starts to shift. When you start thinking about experience, you stop seeing yourself as someone who just delivers work and start seeing yourself as someone who guides the process. You move from doing jobs to playing roles, as a mentor, a creative partner, a trusted voice in the room.

JOBS VS. ROLES

I've been talking about this idea of jobs versus roles for a while now, and every time I bring it up with other creatives, something clicks. It just makes sense.

Jobs are fine. They pay the bills, they give you structure, they look good on LinkedIn. But they're fragile. They can change overnight, disappear without warning, or get replaced by new technology before you've even had your morning coffee. If all your confidence and identity sit inside a job title, it can leave you feeling lost when things shift.

Roles are different. They're the things you naturally bring to whatever you do. Maybe you're the guide, the builder, the storyteller, the explorer, the one who spots opportunities, or the one who keeps everyone calm when things get messy. That's your role. It's who you are when you're at your best.

The beauty of roles is that they move with you. They grow as you grow. They don't vanish when your job changes, and they're what people remember about you long after a project is done. Long before job titles existed, people were known for their roles. The protector, the nurturer, the dreamer, the rebel. Those parts of us are still the same today.

And right now, this mindset really matters. There are going to be more people designing than ever before, but not many who can lead the process with clarity and care. The ones who stand out won't just be the people who make things look good; they'll be the ones who guide, host, and mentor their clients through the journey.

So, if you've ever felt boxed in by a job title or worried about what happens if things change, remember this.

You're not your job.

You're something bigger than that. You bring qualities that can't be replaced by software or stripped away by a title.
You bring a role.

Chapter Fourteen -

MYTH BUSTING THE COMMON BULLSH*T

There are thousands of words floating around in the branding world, and it can be hard to keep track of what they all mean. So, to make life easier, here's a quick guide to the fifty most useful ones.

Think of this as your branding phrasebook—short, simple, and written in normal human language. When these terms come up in conversation, you'll know exactly what they mean and how to use them.

CORE BRAND FOUNDATIONS

1. **Vision** – The big picture of where you're heading
2. **Mission** – What you actually do each day to make that vision happen
3. **Purpose** – The reason you exist that isn't just about money
4. **Values** – The things you believe in and try to live by
5. **Goals** – The big things you want to achieve
6. **Objectives** – The smaller, measurable steps that help you hit those goals
7. **Strategy** – The smart plan for how you'll reach your goals
8. **Tactics** – The practical actions that make the plan real
9. **Value Proposition** – The clear reason someone should choose you
10. **Positioning** – The space you take up in people's minds compared to others
11. **Differentiation** – What makes you stand out in a way that actually matters
12. **Brand Promise** – What people can always expect from you

COMMUNICATION & MESSAGING

13. **Tone of Voice** – How you sound when you speak or write
14. **Messaging Framework** – The main things you need to say, and who you're saying them to
15. **Key Message** – The one thing you want people to remember
16. **Tagline** – A short, lasting line that sums you up
17. **Slogan** – A short line used for a single campaign or promotion
18. **Manifesto** – A statement of what you believe and stand for
19. **Elevator Pitch** – How you explain what you do in thirty seconds or less
20. **Brand Language** – The words and phrases that help you sound consistent
21. **Brand Story** – The journey of how you got here and why you do what you do

AUDIENCE & MARKET

22. **Target Audience** – The people you want to reach
23. **Demographics** – Facts about who they are (age, location, income, and so on)
24. **Psychographics** – What drives them (values, interests, fears)
25. **Persona** – A simple profile of your ideal customer
26. **Customer Journey** – The steps someone takes from discovering you to becoming loyal
27. **Touchpoints** – Every moment someone interacts with your brand

PERSONALITY & PERCEPTION

28. Brand Personality – The human traits people see in you
29. Archetype – The role or character your brand plays (like hero, rebel, explorer)
30. Attributes – The words that describe your style or vibe
31. Perception – How people currently see you
32. Reputation – The collective belief people hold about you
33. Brand Image – The overall picture people hold in their heads
34. Brand Awareness – How many people actually know you exist

VISUAL & VERBAL IDENTITY

35. Logo – The main mark people recognise you by
36. Wordmark – Your name styled as a logo
37. Symbol / Icon – A simple image that represents you
38. Typography – The fonts you use and how you use them
39. Colour Palette – The colours that help people spot you quickly
40. Visual Style – The overall look and feel of your brand
41. Style Guide – The rulebook for keeping everything consistent
42. Creative Direction – The visual plan that ties everything together

GROWTH, ACTION & LONGEVITY

43. Brand Launch – How you introduce your brand to the world
44. Rebrand – Giving your brand a major refresh or full rebuild
45. Campaign – A focused push to promote something specific
46. Content Strategy – The plan for what you make, where you share it, and why
47. Brand Experience – How people feel when they deal with you

BUSINESS & IMPACT

48. Brand Equity – The extra value your name adds because people know and trust you
49. Brand Loyalty – When people stick with you even when they have other options
50. Return on Investment (ROI) – The results you get compared to the time or money you put in

"JUDGE ME FOR HOW GOOD MY GOOD IDEAS ARE, NOT FOR HOW BAD MY BAD IDEAS ARE."

— Ben Affleck

Chapter Fifteen -

YOUR NEW ROLE STARTS HERE

You've made it this far—nice one, mate.

Thanks for sticking with me. Together, we've cut through the noise, questioned the distractions, the language, the mindsets, and started to see branding through a whole new lens. Now, it's time to do something with it.

This is where the book shifts gears from theory to practice. I didn't want this to be another book shouting branding theory at you. I wanted it to give you the tools to become a super-duper useful brand being. Someone who makes things happen, not just talks about them.

The next three sections give you a system you can actually use. Something you can run, sell, and repeat with confidence. It will help you guide your clients through the chaos, find their focus, and turn foggy ideas into brands that make sense.

You're about to learn a three-phase approach that I've used for years with clients. I've simplified it for this book so it works with any client in any industry. The principles we are about to dive into work for products, services, and personal brands.

This is made for people at the start. Ground-freaking-zero. The ones figuring things out and trying to make something real. When bigger budget clients come knocking, you can add layers, but the foundation never changes. Before you pour time, money, and energy into anything, get your Minimum Viable Brand (MVB) into the world and test it with real people. That is how you learn, grow, and build brands that hang around for a long time.

Here is how it works.

PHASE ONE: DISCOVER

Before any visuals, colours, or logos, we ***unlock*** the idea. You will use the Five Idea Keys, a simple set of tools that bring clarity and direction to any project. They help you guide conversations, ask better questions, and uncover what a brand truly stands for before anyone starts designing.

PHASE TWO: DESIGN

Once the idea is clear, it is time to ***assemble*** the goodness. We create the MVB, the simplest and most honest version of a brand that can show up in the world and start building trust.

PHASE THREE: DELIVER.

Now, it is about taking action to ***launch*** your MVB into the world. Take what you have built, put it out there, learn from real people, and help your clients move from idea to first sale without panic.

Three clear phases, where each one builds on the last: Together they form a system that makes you more confident, more consistent, and more valuable. This is how you move from reacting to briefs to leading projects, shaping ideas, and driving creative direction.

Most of the clients you work with over your career will not have massive budgets or big teams. They will be early-stage founders, makers, and dreamers who need help getting started. They need someone who can listen, simplify, and turn their idea into something real. That someone can be you.

This process gives you what you need to do that. Guide with clarity, lead with structure, and create work that builds trust fast for your clients. Do it consistently and you stop chasing dream clients . . . you start creating them. My plan is to have clients chasing you, because you will become the dream designer and Brand Host they have been looking for.

One more little thing before we dive in. Everything in these next sections can be used two ways.

Client Mode is the main focus. It is about helping others make better decisions, showing your leadership, and guiding ideas into reality.

Solo Mode is the bonus. The same tools and questions, but for your own ideas. It is where you test new concepts, explore extra revenue streams, and give yourself space to create and grow on your own terms.

Both matter . . . as I always want you to be working on your own ideas, as well as your clients' ideas.

SAFWAN'S $86K WAKE-UP CALL

Let me tell you about my friend Saf.

He is a genuinely kind and smart human. After more than twenty years in corporate, he finally decided to go all in on his own idea. He had the passion. He had the vision. The idea was a health-tech startup, a wellness app designed to help people live better. On paper, it sounded brilliant. He built the tech, he built the brand, he built the dream. I even helped him develop some of the visual direction.

But eight months later, it was gone. No paying customers. Just a handful of polite beta testers and a lot of feedback that came too late. By that point, Saf had already spent around **$86,000** trying to bring the idea to life . . . money that vanished faster than he ever imagined.

His wake-up call came in one short line from a potential user who said, "This is cool, but I'd never pay for it."

That sentence changed everything for him. It was the moment he realised he hadn't built something people needed. He'd built something he wanted them to want.

Now, this isn't a story about failure. It's a story about what happens when good intentions outpace validation, something we as designers see all the time. A founder gets excited, skips the testing, and rushes to build the brand before the idea has been shaped. And we often get pulled into that same rush with them.

Saf's story is a reminder that, as designers, we're not just here to make things look great. We're here to help our clients think before they build. To slow them down long enough to make sure the thing they're creating actually solves a real problem.

That's one of the main reasons I created the **Five Idea Keys** and the concept of the **MVB**. They exist to stop this exact situation from happening, to give designers a way to guide their clients toward clarity before they pour too much time and money into execution. The Five Idea Keys turn vague passion into structured proof. The MVB gives that proof something real to stand on.

Saf was kind enough to let me share his story because he knows it's not unique. It happens everywhere, every year, to thousands of people who build first and validate later. And it's our job as brand thinkers to help them avoid that trap.

So, when you spot a client caught up in the rush, dreaming big, moving fast, ready to invest before they've tested, this is the moment to pause and guide. Help them shape the idea, test it, and build small before they scale.

That's what the MVB is all about. It's not just a safety net for founders. It's a framework that helps you, the designer, protect your client's time, energy, and investment.

TRUE STORY

Now, to the tool that powers phase one:

The Five Idea Keys

The Five Idea Keys came from years of discovery calls and helping people make sense of their ideas before a single design decision was made. They are simple, practical, and built to do one thing: Unlock clarity. Each key looks at a different part of the idea. Work through them and you get the full picture of what the brand is about, who it is for, and how it should show up. Once that clarity is in place, creative decisions get a lot easier.

The keys give you structured prompts and simple exercises that turn vague thoughts into shared language and clear direction. They were created to make design and strategic conversations easy to understand for everyone. We know by now how much language matters, friends. The way we talk about ideas dictates how people feel about them.

The Five Idea Keys make those conversations fun, human, and accessible. They help clients feel included and confident . . . you do not need fancy words or fluffy words to sound smart. Your clear communication proves you know what you are doing. The result is less confusion, faster progress, and a client who feels part of the process. You move from talking in circles to making decisions with confidence.

Over the next few chapters, you will see how each key fits together and what its role is in the process. From my twenty years in this industry, I can tell you that once you understand these keys, you will be able to shape an MVB that is genuinely effective: a brand built with intention from the start, one that has every chance of lasting.

At its core, this is about giving clients what they actually need right now, not what we think they should have. It is easy to fall into the trap of offering the same set of deliverables everyone else does because it looks impressive. The MVB approach cuts through that. It helps you give people exactly what they need at the stage they are at, not a bloated package built to pad a portfolio. Meet people where they are, keep it simple, and build something that can grow over time.

That is the beauty of it. It is not about showing off; it is about showing up. It is about helping people move forward with clarity, confidence, and something real to build from.

That is where we are heading next.
It is time to learn how to unlock ideas.
Let's get into the Five Idea Keys.

Lincoln Patches

SECTION THREE

THE FIVE IDEA KEYS FRAMEWORK

The Five Idea Keys started as my MVB. For years, it was something I tested, validated, and shared quietly with friends, clients, and people I coached. It wasn't a framework at first—just a way of thinking that helped me make sense of ideas before they turned into projects.

After thousands of hours on client calls, I realized discovery needed to change. Too often it felt stiff and one-sided, more like a boring Q&A than the start of a creative partnership. So, I began making those early conversations lighter and more workshop-style, adding simple exercises and keeping the language accessible.

The shift was immediate . . . clients relaxed, clarity came quicker, and projects started with far better energy. Over time I realised the process could stand on its own. It could be shared with people who couldn't afford my services, or who weren't quite ready for full studio work yet. That's when the Five Idea Keys grew beyond me. What started as a personal tool became PDFs, then mini-courses, and eventually an ecosystem designed to help people shape ideas properly from the start.

I genuinely believe that the more ideas get actioned and built, the more opportunities there are for designers, creators, and founders to do meaningful work and live the lives they want to live. The Five Idea Keys is now a tool for EVERYONE, and that makes me proud.

Let's go, team.

2
LINCOLN DESIGN CO.
Lincoln
DESIGN

INTRODUCTION TO THE KEYS

Every strong brand begins with an idea. But between the excitement of a new spark and the reality of bringing it to life, most ideas lose shape. They grow messy, get rushed, or become overcomplicated long before they ever reach the world. The Five Idea Keys exist to prevent that from happening.

This framework guides you step by step through the early stages of shaping an idea. It's a sequential process where each key opens the next stage of development. You start by understanding your Spark, then move through the People and Place that surround it, define how it feels through Energy, and finish by shaping what it delivers through your Offer.

Used in order, the keys bring structure and confidence to the uncertain space between idea and brand. They give you a way to make sense of creative chaos, to ask better questions, and to find clarity before committing to design. Whether you're working alone or with a client, the process helps you uncover meaning, direction, and focus.

Most of the time, you'll use this in *client mode*. It's designed for discovery calls and brand workshops, the conversations that set the tone for everything that follows. Each key includes practical prompts and exercises that help you draw out the insights you need to move a project forward with purpose. But the framework is just as powerful in *solo mode*, when you're shaping your own idea or testing something new.

Think of the Five Idea Keys as a permanent tool in your creative tool kit. They're a repeatable way to make sense of any idea and a framework you can return to again and again throughout your career.

The reason this system uses colour and the language of keys is simple: accessibility.

"Brand strategy" can easily become abstract, heavy, and full of jargon that leaves clients feeling uncertain or disconnected from their own ideas.

The Five Idea Keys strip that complexity away. Each one is visual, memorable, and built around plain-language conversations that anyone can follow. This means you can walk a client through important strategic decisions without intimidating them.

SPARK
Clarifies why you exist.

PERSON
Defines who you serve.

PLACE
Understands where you belong.

ENERGY
Decides how you show up.

OFFER
Shapes what you deliver.

The colours create recognition, the metaphor of keys suggests progress and unlocking, and the structure builds confidence on both sides of the table.

As a designer, you gain a clear framework to guide discovery. As a client, they get a process they can understand and trust. It bridges the gap between creative thinking and clear communication, turning early brand conversations into something people can actually grasp and get really excited about . . . this helps you become the Brand Host and creative partner.

We will go into all of these in more detail over the next section of the book but, together, the Five Idea Keys form a complete decision-making system. They give structure to intuition, bringing order to the early stages of creativity and turning loose ideas into brands that make sense.

Once you have completed the keys with your clients, you can add it all into a ShapeDoc that you can send to your clients after the Discover part of your project . . . get this signed off with them before you start designing.

Let's get into it.

P.S. If you want to learn more about the Five Idea Keys, MVBs, or how to build reputations that become successful brands, then scan the QR code below. I have added in a load of extra material and resources.

The Spark

Chapter Sixteen —

THE RED KEY: THE SPARK

The moment that started it all and the mission it set in motion.

WHY THE RED KEY MATTERS

Every idea starts somewhere. A spark, a thought, a moment when something just clicked. But as time passes and things develop, that original moment can get lost in the noise. The Red Key helps you come back to that moment—the reason it began in the first place.

When you start a discovery session with your clients, asking about where the idea came from is one of the easiest ways to open the conversation. It's relaxed, it's human, and it gives people a natural starting point. Everyone has a story behind why they started something, and when they begin to talk about it, they usually light up.

This isn't about writing a mission statement or finding perfect words. It's about uncovering what really matters to them and why they care enough to build this thing. That moment usually holds all the truth and emotion you need to guide the rest of the brand.

Once you've found that spark, everything else becomes clearer. The visuals, the tone, the direction—all of it starts to line up. It gives you a strong foundation to build from and gives your client confidence because they can see the meaning behind what they're creating.

USING THE RED KEY IN DISCOVERY

Objective: Open a natural conversation that helps you uncover one clear Spark Line.

Discovery Call or Workshop Flow

1. Invite the story: "Where did this start for you?" "What happened that made this real?"

2. Find the meaning: "Why did that matter to you?" "What changed after that moment?"

3. Name the mission: "What do you want to change for others because of this?"

As they talk, listen for specific moments, emotional words, and patterns that keep coming up. When you notice a thread, reflect it back by saying, "It sounds like this started when . . ." If they nod or light up, you've found the Spark.

After the call, take what you heard and shape it into one short paragraph called a Spark Line. You don't need to send it yet. It becomes one of the five parts of your ShapeDoc, the summary you'll share with your client once all the keys are complete. It makes sure everyone's aligned before you start designing.

You can find templates and examples by scanning the QR code on page 113.

WHAT THE RED KEY UNLOCKS

The Red Key helps you uncover the story behind the idea, the real reason it exists. By taking the time to talk through where it began, you'll help your client reconnect with their original Spark and see their idea with fresh clarity.

When you read it back together, it should feel like the kind of story that makes them nod and say, "That's exactly why I started this."

HOW TO USE THE SPARK LADDER

Once you've finished the discovery session, take your notes and pull out the main phrases or moments that stood out. You're looking for the thread that ties it all together, the "aha" moment that explains why this whole thing started.

From there, use the three Spark Ladder steps to build a short paragraph that captures that moment, why it mattered, and what it set in motion. Keep it natural, not polished. You can always refine it later.

Encourage your client to read it out loud. If it feels true to them and they light up when they hear it, you've found the Spark.

RED KEY EXERCISE:

Once you've found that Spark, it's time to turn it into something clear and simple. That's where the Spark Ladder comes in. It moves you from moment to mission in three simple steps and gives you the Spark Line.

Step 1: What happened?
Find the moment. What happened that made this idea impossible to ignore?

Step 2: Why did it matter?
Dig into the feeling. Why did that moment stay with you?

Step 3: What's going to change because of it?
Define the mission. What do you want to change for others because of that moment?

Now, bring your answers together into one short paragraph.

Framework
This idea came to me when **[answer to Step 1].**
It mattered to me because **[answer to Step 2].**
Now I want to build something that will **[answer to Step 3].**

Example:
My Personal Spark Line for the Five Idea Keys
"This idea came to me when I noticed founders rushing through the early stages of branding. It mattered to me because I hated watching them lose confidence and waste money. Now I want to build something that will help them shape their ideas before they brand them."

The Spark
The Spark
The Spark

HOW THE RED KEY FEEDS THE MVB

The Spark is the foundation of everything that comes next. It's the heartbeat of your client's brand. Once you've helped them uncover that story, you've given them something a lot of people skip—a clear understanding of why they're doing this in the first place.

For you as a designer, this becomes the anchor for every creative decision that follows. When the Spark is clear, you can design with confidence because you know what it all connects back to.

Once this stage is complete, you're ready to move outward and explore the Blue Key: the Person. That's where you'll identify the human this brand is built for and start connecting the Spark to someone who actually needs it.

OTHER QUESTIONS YOU CAN ASK

- What made this idea impossible to ignore?
- When did it first feel real?
- What moment changed how you saw things?
- Why did that matter to you personally?
- What do you want to change because of it?

OUTPUT

Deliverable: A completed Spark Line: a short paragraph that captures how and why the idea began. This becomes one of the five parts of the ShapeDoc, sitting alongside the Person, Place, Energy, and Offer. It's the foundation everything else connects back to.

STEP ONE
WHAT HAPPENED?

STEP TWO
WHY DID IT MATTER?

STEP THREE
WHAT IS GOING TO CHANGE BECAUSE OF IT?

YOUR SPARK LINE

TIP

If your client struggles to remember the exact moment their idea came to them, ask them to describe what was happening in their life around that time. Often, they'll stumble into it naturally while talking about what frustrated or inspired them.

You can also ask,
"When did this idea stop being just a thought and start feeling real?"

That question usually unlocks the truth.

The Person

Chapter Seventeen –

THE BLUE KEY: THE PERSON

The person your idea is built for and what they truly need.

WHY THE BLUE KEY MATTERS

Every brand exists to serve someone. If it doesn't, you're not building a brand . . . you're just making something for yourself. Before you can design for those people, you need to know who they are beyond the obvious stuff.

The Blue Key is about finding the human in the middle of it all, the person your client's idea is built for. This isn't about creating a made-up target audience. It's about empathy. You're helping your client see their audience as a real person with a life, emotions, goals, frustrations, and needs.

When you use the Blue Key in discovery, you start uncovering what really connects the brand to that person. You'll hear the words they use, notice what matters most to them, and see how the brand can genuinely make a difference in their day-to-day life. Once your client can clearly picture that person, every creative decision becomes easier.

USING THE BLUE KEY IN DISCOVERY

Objective: Uncover the one real person your client's idea is built for and understand what they need most.

Discovery Call or Workshop Flow

1. Find the human: Ask "Who is this really for?" or "If you had to picture one person using this, who would it be?"

2. Understand their world: Ask "What does their day look like?" "What do they love?" "What frustrates them?" and "What do they care about most?"

3. Clarify the connection: Ask "How does your idea make their life better or easier?" or "Why would they choose this over something else?"

As you chat, listen for clues that reveal emotions and behaviours rather than surface-level facts. The goal isn't to create a perfect customer profile. It's to start seeing the world through this person's eyes. When you can picture what's in their kitchen, what podcasts they listen to, or what they do on a Saturday morning, you're onto the good stuff.

After the call, take what you've heard and turn it into a one-page profile called the Person ID Sheet. Give the Person a name, a few key details, and a bit of personality. You don't need to send it yet. It will become one of the five parts of your ShapeDoc, the summary you'll share once all the keys are complete to make sure everyone's aligned before you start designing.

You can find templates and examples by scanning the QR code on page 113.

WHAT THE BLUE KEY UNLOCKS

The Blue Key helps you humanise the brand. By understanding who the idea is truly for, you give the brand something to connect to.

When you show your client their Person ID Sheet, it should feel real. You don't want them to see a generic persona; you want them to see someone they could talk to. Sometimes the Person they describe might even sound like them, or maybe it's a close friend. That's perfectly fine. In fact, it's usually a sign the idea is rooted in something personal, which is exactly where great brands come from.

When your client can point at that page and say, "That's who we're building for," everything starts to click.

BLUE KEY EXERCISE

THE PERSON ID SHEET

This is where you help your client turn their thoughts into something visual and memorable.

The Person ID Sheet is a simple one-page snapshot of who the brand is built for. It's a human reference point, something your client can print out, stick on their wall, and use to keep every decision focused on the person who matters most.

Here's how to run it in a call or workshop.

1. Find the human: Ask your client to think of one real person this idea is built for. It might be a past customer, a friend, or even someone in their family. If they can picture them clearly, you're already halfway there.

2. Bring them to life: Have a relaxed chat using the questions below. Keep it natural. You're just trying to paint a believable picture of this person's life and what they care about.

3. Capture the essentials: When you're done, pull together the key points into a simple one-page Person ID Sheet.

Person ID Sheet Prompts and Guiding Questions

1. Name: What would you call this person?

2. Age and stage of life: Roughly how old are they and what's happening in their life right now?

3. Where they're based: Where do they live or spend most of their time?

4. Job or role: What do they do for work or passion?

5. Goals: What are they trying to achieve in life or work?

6. Frustrations: What slows them down or stresses them out?

7. Motivations: What keeps them going? What excites or drives them?

8. Decision drivers: What helps them choose between options?

9. Hobbies or interests: What do they do for fun or to unwind?

10. Income band (optional): Do they have disposable income? Are they careful with money or more spontaneous?

Once you've filled this in, you should be able to picture the Person like a real person. If you can describe what they'd say in a conversation or how they'd react to something, you've done it right.

HOW THE BLUE KEY FEEDS THE MVB

Once you know who the brand is built for, every creative decision becomes clearer. Every colour, every word, every offer connects back to this Person. For your client, this removes the guesswork. It helps them stop designing for everyone and start building something that actually resonates with the right people.

For you as a designer, it gives every part of your process a face to design for. You're no longer creating for a foggy audience. You're designing for a real human being with a story, emotions, and needs.

Once the Person ID Sheet is complete, you're ready to move on to the Green Key: the Place. This is where you'll explore the Place your client's idea belongs in the world and how it fits within its environment.

OTHER QUESTIONS YOU CAN ASK

- Who is this really for?
- What's their story?
- What do they wish was easier right now?
- What are they afraid of getting wrong?
- How do you want them to feel after they've worked with you or used your product?
- What would a great day look like for them?

OUTPUT

Deliverable: A completed Person ID Sheet: a simple one-page profile that brings the audience to life. It will sit in the ShapeDoc alongside the other four keys.

TIP

If your client struggles to answer, ask if there's someone in their close friendship group who this would be perfect for.

Once they have that person in mind, get them to describe them. It helps make the exercise feel easier. We all know our friends.

HOW TO USE THE SHEET

Encourage your client to keep the sheet visible, printed, pinned up, or saved on their desktop. Every creative choice should serve this Person. If it doesn't, it probably doesn't serve the brand.

IMAGE

NAME

AGE

WHERE THEY LIVE

GOALS

JOB

FRUSTRATIONS

MOTIVATIONS

HOBBIES

DECISION DRIVERS

INCOME

The Place

Chapter Eighteen –

THE GREEN KEY: THE PLACE

The environment your idea lives in and how it fits within the world around it.

WHY THE GREEN KEY MATTERS

Every idea exists in an environment, whether that's online or out in the real world. There's always a landscape, a context, and a set of people already doing something similar. The Green Key helps you and your client understand that world clearly so the brand can find its own Place within it.

This isn't about copying or competing. It's about alignment and awareness. When your client can see the Place they're stepping into, they can start to make smarter decisions about how to stand out rather than blend in.

Most clients have a rough sense of who their competitors are, but they rarely look at them properly. They might admire or compare, but not analyse in a way that actually helps to position them better. The Green Key gives them a simple structure for doing that, helping them see what works, what doesn't, and where they might fit best. Once they can visualise that Place, the brand starts to feel more intentional and a lot less accidental.

USING THE GREEN KEY IN DISCOVERY

Objective: Help your client understand where their brand sits in the current landscape and how it differs from others in their place.

Discovery Call or Workshop Flow

1. Explore the space: Ask "Who else is doing something similar to you?" or "Who would your perfect person compare you to?"

2. Understand perception: Ask "How do those brands feel?" "What makes them stand out?" and "What do you think they do well or miss completely?"

3. Find your place: Ask "If we put all of these brands on a map, where would you land?" "Do you see yourself sitting closer to this one or that one?" and "Who do you feel most similar to right now?"

Encourage your client to look at their competitors with curiosity rather than judgment. This isn't about who's better or worse. It's about identifying the qualities that make each brand feel a certain way and understanding where theirs naturally fits.

After the call, help your client map out this information visually using the Environment Axis. This tool lets them see where they sit and how they compare to others, giving both of you a shared reference point before you start designing.

It becomes one of the five parts of your ShapeDoc, the summary you'll share once all the keys are complete.

You can find templates and examples by scanning the QR code on page 113.

WHAT THE GREEN KEY UNLOCKS

The Green Key brings context to your client's brand. It helps them understand the environment they're stepping into and the place they can own.

When you show your client their Environment Axis, it should help them see their unique position clearly. They'll be able to recognise which brands cluster together and where there's space to stand apart. That realisation builds confidence. It helps them see that their brand has a defined Place in the world, and that clarity gives you a strong foundation to design from.

GREEN KEY EXERCISE

THE ENVIRONMENT AXIS

The Environment Axis helps your client visualise the place their brand lives in. It's a simple grid that compares brands by price and personality.

On one axis, you have Affordable to Expensive, and on the other, you have Playful to Serious. These two dimensions work for almost any brand and are simple enough for clients to understand straight away. Here's how to run it in a call or workshop.

1. Plot the landscape: Ask your client to pick three other brands or businesses in their place. These could be local competitors, national chains, or even brands from other industries that feel relevant to what they're building.

2. Place them on the map: Draw the two axes and label them Playful to Serious and Affordable to Expensive. Then ask your client to mark an X for each competitor based on how they feel. Encourage them to trust their gut. This isn't about right or wrong answers, it's about how the brands are perceived.

3. Plot their own brand: Now, get your client to place themselves on the same map. Where do they sit right now, and where would they like to move toward? This gives you both a quick snapshot of how their brand feels and where it could evolve.

Once the axis is complete, take a photo or save a digital copy to include in the ShapeDoc. It becomes a visual reference point for tone, price perception, and positioning.

The Place

The Place

HOW THE GREEN KEY FEEDS THE MVB

The Green Key gives you the context you need to design with purpose. It stops you from working in isolation and grounds your ideas in the real world.

For your client, it's often the first time they've seen their market mapped out clearly. It removes confusion and helps them understand their positioning in a way that feels simple and visual.

For you as a designer, it means you're not guessing. You're designing with intent, and you know exactly where the brand sits and how it can stand out.

Once the Environment Axis is complete, you're ready to move on to the Yellow Key: the Energy. That's where you'll define the brand's energy, tone, and personality . . . the feeling that makes it recognisable.

EXAMPLE: COFFEE BRANDS ON THE ENVIRONMENT AXIS

Imagine you're working with a coffee shop client. You could plot a few well-known brands to show how this works in practice.

- Blue Bottle Coffee: Expensive and serious, very premium and minimalist
- Grind: Expensive but playful, stylish, and modern with a fun edge
- Costa Coffee: Midrange and serious, reliable, and consistent
- Starbucks: Midrange and slightly playful, global, and lifestyle driven
- Craft Accords (from the earlier case study): Affordable and playful, creative, local, and community led

HOW TO USE THE ENVIRONMENT AXIS

You can refer back to it throughout the process. It's especially useful when you're making creative decisions about tone, colour, materials, or messaging. Everything should make sense in the position your client has chosen.

OTHER QUESTIONS YOU CAN ASK

- Who are your top three competitors?
- Which brands do you admire, even if they're not in your industry?
- How do you want people to perceive your brand next to these?
- Where do you feel there's a gap or opportunity?
- If your brand were a person walking into a room full of competitors, how would it stand out?

TIP

Encourage honesty. It's better for clients to plot where they are now rather than where they want to be.

Once you both understand the truth of their current position, you can design a path that helps them move closer to where they want to go.

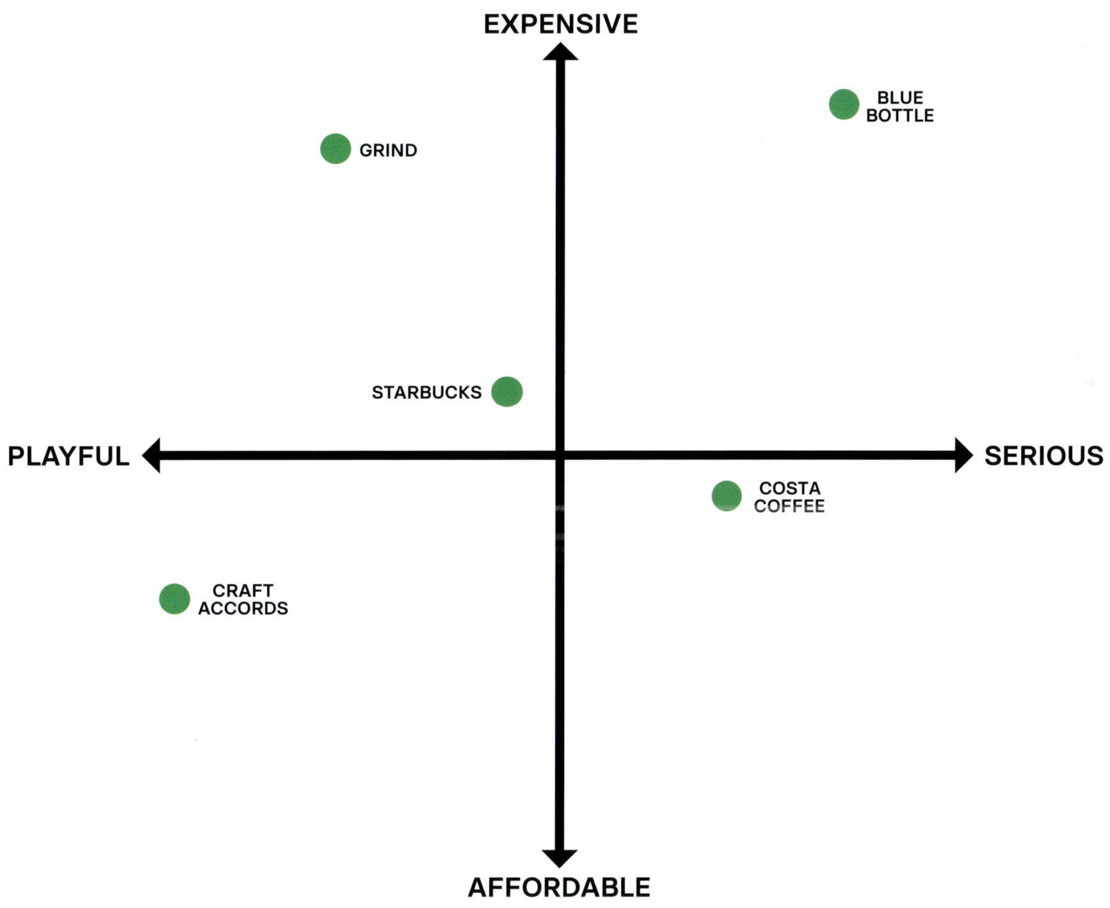

the Energy

Chapter Nineteen –

THE YELLOW KEY: THE ENERGY

The energy, tone, and personality that make your brand recognisable.

WHY THE YELLOW KEY MATTERS

All brands give off a certain energy. You can feel it in how they speak, how they behave, and how they look. That energy shapes how people connect with them, often before a single word of copy or design choice has been made.

The Yellow Key is about finding that Energy. It helps you and your client figure out how the brand should feel so every creative decision has direction and purpose. Once this Energy is defined, the visuals, tone, and messaging all start to flow naturally.

When you're working with clients, this is usually one of the most enjoyable parts of discovery. It's where things start to come alive. You get to talk about personality, style, and behaviour in a way that's fun, approachable, and full of insight. It's not about being perfect or ticking boxes; it's about finding the feeling that makes the brand feel human.

Your goal here is simple. Help your client define how they sound, how they behave, and how they look. These three pieces of the puzzle make up the Energy Map, a visual snapshot of the brand's personality that connects how it communicates with how it presents itself.

USING THE YELLOW KEY IN DISCOVERY

Objective: Uncover the brand's tone, behaviour, and personality so you can capture how it should sound, act, and look.

Discovery Call or Workshop Flow

1. Start with conversation: Ask "How do you want people to feel when they interact with your brand?" or "If your brand walked into a room, how would it come across?"

2. Explore behaviour: Ask "What do you believe in?" or "How do you want people to describe working with you?"

3. Talk visuals: Ask "What kind of energy do you want your visuals to give off?" or "What brands do you admire visually, and why?"

As your client talks, listen for patterns in the words they use. You'll start hearing certain traits repeating, such as "warm," "bold," "calm," "confident," or "curious." These become clues that help you define their brand's energy.

You don't need to finalise anything on the call. Take notes, ask questions, and capture the essence of what you hear. Later, you'll use these insights to build the Energy Map, which will sit as one of the five parts of your ShapeDoc.

You can download templates and examples at by scanning the QR code on page 113.

WHAT THE YELLOW KEY UNLOCKS

The Yellow Key brings emotion and character into the process. It helps your client see their brand as something with a personality, not just a product or service.

When you show your client their Energy Map, it should feel familiar. They should look at it and say, "Yes, that's us." That moment of recognition is what makes this step powerful. It bridges the gap between strategy and creativity, turning abstract ideas into something people can actually feel.

YELLOW KEY EXERCISE

THE ENERGY MAP

The Energy Map helps your client define their brand's Energy in three simple parts. Keep it light and quick. Aim for three words or traits in each circle. Any more than that and it starts to get muddy. Here's how to run it in a call or workshop.

1. How they sound:
This is all about voice and tone. Ask questions like:

* How do you want people to feel when they hear from you?
* What kind of tone feels right: calm, confident, playful, bold?
* If your brand was a person, how would they talk?

What words or phrases already feel natural to you?

Your client is not trying to sound like someone else. You're helping your client sound like themselves.

2. How they behave:
This is where values show up in action. Ask:

* What do you believe in?
* How do you treat your clients or customers?
* How do you want people to describe working with you?
* What do you do differently from others in your space?

These answers show how the brand behaves in the world and how it earns trust.

3. How they look:
This is about translating that energy visually. Ask:

* What kind of feeling should your visuals give off: calm and minimal; bold and expressive; clean and modern?
* What brands do you visually admire?
* What colours, textures, or materials feel right for you?
* What would instantly make you say, "That's not us"?

Once you've gone through all three, you'll start to see patterns and overlaps.

The circles "Sound" and "Behave" form the foundation of the verbal identity. The circles "Behave" and "Look" form the foundation of the visual identity.

It's not a big strategic process. It's just a starting point, but it gives you and your client something solid to build from. It's an easy way to make sure that how the brand sounds and looks always connects back to how it behaves.

HOW TO USE THE ENERGY MAP

Once you've gathered your notes from the call or workshop, take a bit of time to shape them into an Energy Map. Keep it simple. Choose no more than three traits for each circle: "Sound," "Behave," and "Look."

These three sets of words will form one of the five parts of your ShapeDoc. It doesn't need to be perfect; it just needs to feel true to what you heard. The goal is to give both you and your client a clear creative direction that connects tone, behaviour, and visuals.

Keep it simple and natural. You're not writing a set of rules, you're describing a feeling.

OUTPUT

Deliverable: A completed Energy Map: a visual snapshot of how the brand sounds, behaves, and looks. It will sit in the ShapeDoc alongside the other four keys.

EXAMPLE ENERGY MAP

Sound: confident, warm, conversational
Behave: curious, kind, consistent
Look: bold, friendly, handmade

OTHER QUESTIONS YOU CAN ASK

If the conversation ever slows down or your client needs a nudge, try a few of these:

- ✷ How do you want people to describe your brand in three words?
- ✷ What kind of energy do you bring into a room?
- ✷ If your brand had a theme song, what would it be?
- ✷ What would never feel like you?

These kinds of questions often help people loosen up and think more instinctively.

HOW THE YELLOW KEY FEEDS THE MVB

The Yellow Key defines the energy that ties the MVB together. It connects strategy to creativity and gives meaning to every design choice.

When the Energy Map is clear, the MVB feels alive. It doesn't just look right—it feels right.

Once this stage is complete, you're ready to move on to the Black Key: the Offer. That's where you'll define the Offer: The product, service, or experience that brings all this energy to life.

TIP

You don't need to build the Energy Map live with your client. You can create it after the call using your notes from the conversation. It's often easier that way because you can step back, spot patterns, and capture their true energy without overcomplicating it.

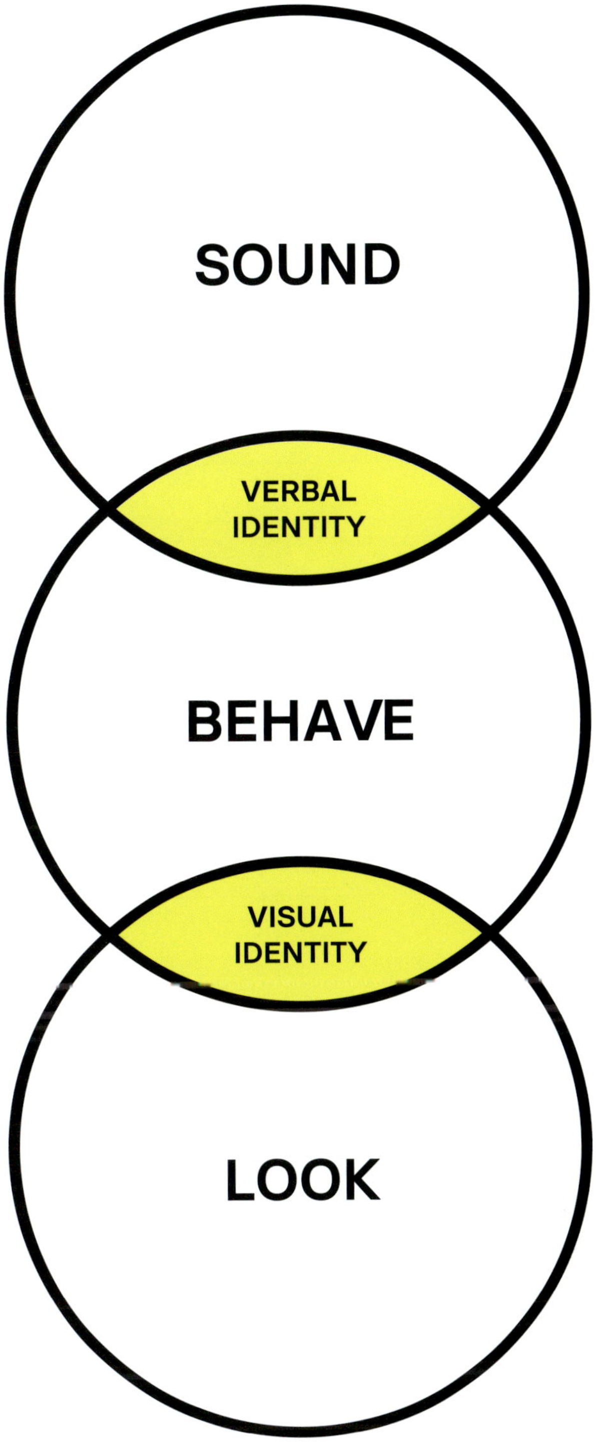

The Offer

Chapter Twenty –

THE BLACK KEY: THE OFFER

The products, services, and experiences that bring your brand to life.

WHY THE BLACK KEY MATTERS

This is the moment where everything you've shaped so far becomes real. By now, you've defined why the brand exists, who it's for, where it belongs, and how it feels. The final step is to define what it actually offers. The Black Key is about clarity, turning ideas into something people can see, touch, and enjoy.

It's not just about listing products or services. It's about shaping what your client gives to the world in a way that connects back to everything you've uncovered. When your client understands what they're really offering and how it makes people feel, it gives the brand direction and gives them confidence to stand behind it.

That's what makes this step powerful. You're helping your client turn intention into action.

WHAT THE BLACK KEY UNLOCKS

The Black Key gives the idea spine. It turns clarity into confidence. By defining boundaries and commitments, it helps your client understand what they're really standing behind. That clarity reduces hesitation. It makes pricing, messaging, and decisions easier. It helps the brand feel deliberate rather than provisional.

When the Black Key is complete, your client can see their idea clearly, explain it simply, and commit to it fully. That conviction creates trust and gives you a solid foundation to design from.

Be sure to check out the sidebar on this page for a full breakdown of what the ShapeDoc includes and how to use it.

USING THE BLACK KEY IN DISCOVERY

Objective: Help your client turn their idea into a clear, intentional offer by defining what it is, who it's for, and what it commits to. The Black Key exists to remove vagueness and make the idea choosable.

Discovery Call or Workshop Flow

1. Get clear on the offer
Ask "What are you really helping people with?" or "When someone chooses you, what are they actually buying?" or "How would you explain this to a friend in one simple sentence?"

2. Understand the edges
Ask "Who is this best suited for, and who probably wouldn't enjoy it?" or "When would this not be the right fit?" or "What kind of work do you want less of?"

3. Agree on what you're standing behind
Ask "What do you want people to be able to rely on every time?" or "What feels important to protect here?" or "What are you happy to say no to so this stays strong?"

Encourage your client to see these decisions as focus, not restriction. The Black Key isn't about limiting the idea. It's about giving it weight and removing uncertainty for the people choosing it.

After the call, help your client capture these decisions in a clear Offer Definition. This becomes one of the five parts of the ShapeDoc, anchoring everything that follows to a real, intentional commitment rather than a loose idea.

You can find templates and examples by scanning the QR code on page 113.

HOW THE FIVE KEYS CONNECT

Each key in this system builds on the one before it. By the time you reach this stage, everything connects like a chain:

Key	Question It Answers	What it gives you
Red Key: Spark	Why does this exist?	Purpose
Blue Key: Person	Who is this for?	Audience
Green Key: Place	Where does it belong?	Context
Yellow Key: Energy	How does it behave?	Character
Black Key: Offer	What does it do?	Delivery

Together, these keys create a complete picture of the idea.
The Red Key gives you the why, the Blue Key gives you the who, the Green Key gives you the where, the Yellow Key gives you the how, and the Black Key ties it all together with the what.

The Offer Stack is where all of those answers meet. It's how you take everything your client has shared and translate it into something people can buy, join, or experience.

BLACK KEY EXERCISE

THE OFFER STACK

The Offer Stack helps you define what your client gives to the world in three simple layers. Each one builds on the next, moving from purpose to delivery to feeling.

You can sketch it as a simple pyramid with three boxes.

Top Layer: The Promise
Why it exists—the emotional or transformational reason behind the Offer. (This connects back to the Spark, the mission behind the brand.) Ask:

* What change are you helping people create in their lives?
* Why does this matter to them?
* What do they gain emotionally when they engage with you?

Middle Layer: The Give
What you actually provide—the tangible product, service, or experience that brings the promise to life. (This connects to the Energy, how it's delivered and expressed.) Ask:

* What do people physically get from you?
* What are your main products or services?
* How do you deliver or share them?

Bottom Layer: The Result
The lasting impression people walk away with. (This connects to the person: how they feel or what changes for them.) Ask:

* How do you want people to feel after working with you or visiting you?
* What should they remember most?
* What do you want them to tell a friend?

When you read the three layers from top to bottom, it tells the full story of the brand in a way that feels real, clear, and human. It's not just what they sell; it's what they give, deliver, and make people feel.

THE OFFER LINE

Once you've written the three layers, you can combine them into one clear, simple sentence using this framework:

"We [Promise] by [Give], so that people can [Result]."

This single line gives your client a natural way to describe what they do without getting too fluffy or overcomplicating it. The Offer Line becomes the starting point for your brand's voice. In section four, we'll take this sentence and expand it into headlines, social bios, and other pieces of real-world messaging.

HOW TO USE THE OFFER STACK

Once you've gathered your notes, shape them into the three layers of the Offer Stack and write one Offer Line that ties them together. Keep each layer short: two or three lines max.

If your client has multiple Offers, that's fine. Group them under the Give but keep one shared Promise and one shared Result. That keeps the story consistent without making it complicated.

Encourage your client to print out the Offer Stack, add it to the wall, or keep it open beside them when they work on messaging. It's a simple way to make sure everything they say or do connects back to what they actually offer.

OTHER QUESTIONS YOU CAN ASK

• What do people thank you for most?
• If you could only offer one thing, what would it be?
• What part of your offer creates the biggest joy or impact?
• Who else offers something similar, and how are you different?
• What do you want people to say about you after they've worked with you?

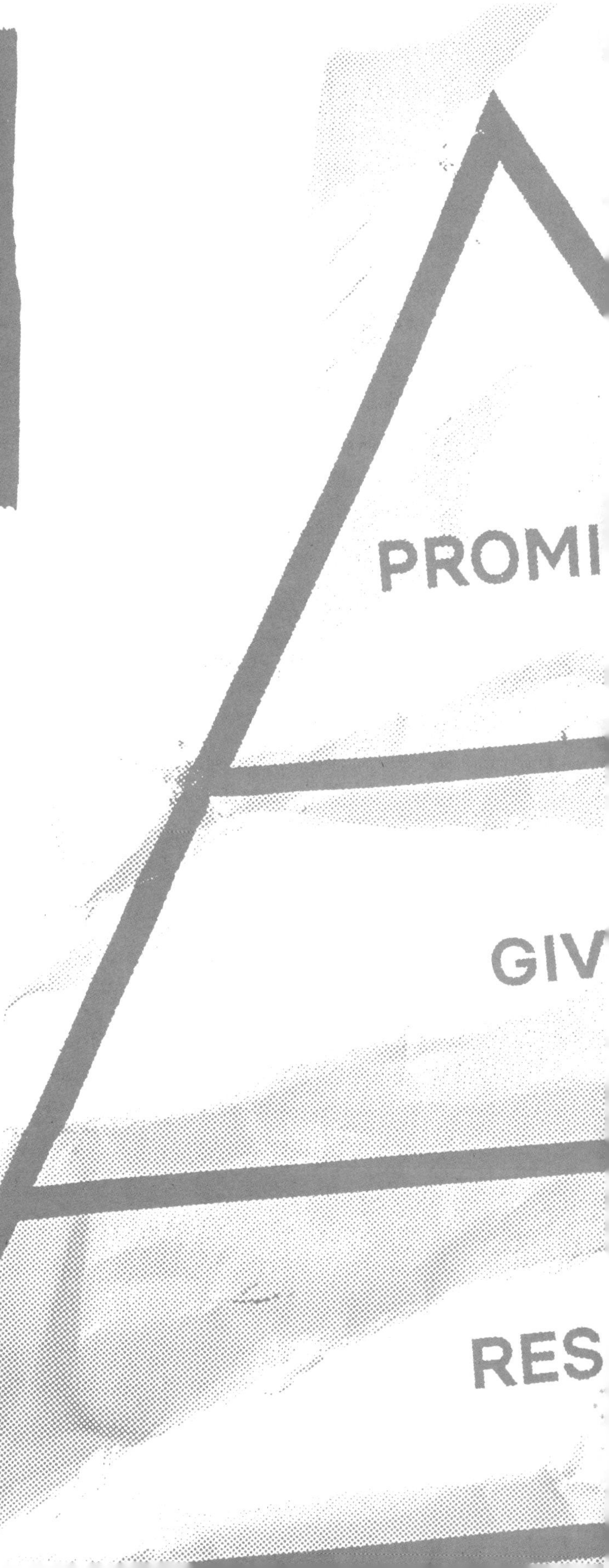

EXAMPLE: COFFEE SHOP

Promise
To give people a calm moment in their day. Life moves fast, and we want to be a space where they can slow down, reconnect, and breathe.

Give
We serve great coffee, handmade pastries, and warm service that makes daily life feel more personal.

Result
People leave feeling grounded, refreshed, and ready to take on the rest of their day.

Offer Line
We help people slow down and reconnect by serving great coffee, handmade pastries, and calm, intentional spaces so they can leave feeling grounded, seen, and ready to take on the rest of their day.

HOW THE BLACK KEY FEEDS THE MVB

The Black Key turns clarity into action. It defines what your client actually does and closes the loop between all the keys.

Now the Five Idea Keys are complete. You've clarified the Spark, the Person, the Place, the Energy, and the Offer.

You're ready to bring them together into the ShapeDoc, the summary you'll share with your client before building their MVB.

Be sure to check out the sidebar on this page for a full breakdown of what the ShapeDoc includes and how to use it.

OUTPUT

Deliverable: A completed Offer Stack with the three layers (Promise, Give, and Result) and an optional Offer Line that ties it all together in one clear sentence. This becomes the final piece of the ShapeDoc, the summary that brings all five keys together before design begins.

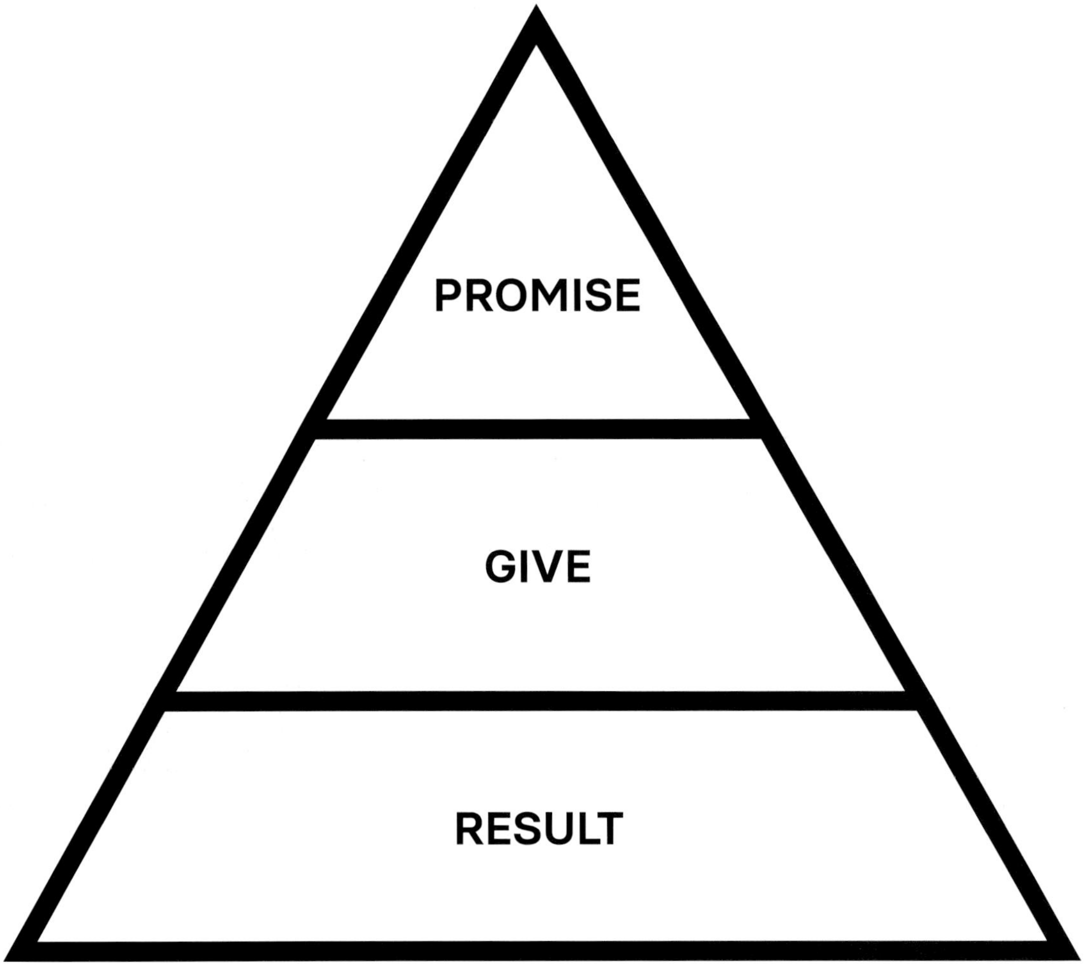

TIP

When you're helping your client with this, keep the language simple and human.

They don't need a long list or perfect wording. They just need to be clear on three things—what they promise, what they give, and how people feel as a result.

If those three parts feel honest and true, they've done it right.

SHAPEDOC

The ShapeDoc is the thing that pulls everything together. After you've worked through the Five Idea Keys, you'll have pages of notes and insights floating around. The ShapeDoc turns all that into one clear, simple document your client can actually understand.

It's not a strategy deck or a big presentation. It's a short summary that captures everything you've uncovered—the Spark, the Person, the Place, the Energy, and the Offer. It's what you and your client can point to and say, "This is what we're building."

You can make it as a clean PDF, a Notion page, or even a Google Doc or use the template I have supplied on the resources folder. The format doesn't matter. What matters is that it's shared and signed off on before you start designing. That small step gives you and your client a shared foundation to build from.

The ShapeDoc gives you a few powerful things.

Alignment
It makes sure you and your client are on the same page before you open Illustrator or start sketching. Everyone knows what's being built and why, which saves you from endless back-and-forth later.

Confidence
For your client, it's proof that you've really listened. Seeing their words and ideas reflected clearly builds trust. It shows you understand them, and that makes them feel safe putting their brand in your hands.

Direction
When you start designing, the ShapeDoc becomes your guide. Every logo, colour, or type choice can be traced back to something in it. That makes your creative decisions easy to explain and hard to argue with.

I'd always suggest getting the ShapeDoc signed off on before moving forward. It doesn't need to be formal. A simple "Yes, this feels right" is enough. That moment of agreement gives you both confidence and clarity.

The ShapeDoc is a small step that changes everything. It keeps you aligned, helps your client trust you, and turns discovery into direction. It's where the real work of brand building begins.

You can find templates and examples by scanning the QR code on page 113.

SECTION FOUR

BUILDING YOUR MVB

By this point, you've got the groundwork sorted. You know the Five Idea Keys. You've learned how to dig through the mess, pull out what matters, and uncover the meaning behind an idea during a client workshop or discovery call.

Now comes the fun bit: the designer's playground, where we take everything you've uncovered and turn it into something visual.

This is where we start thinking creatively again, but with a new kind of focus. Instead of guessing, overcomplicating, or exploring fourteen different logo directions just for the sake of it, this stage is about taking what you already know and using it to build something simple, smart, and solid that your client can actually use to get going.

Ultimately, we are going to look at how the Five Idea Keys translate into real design decisions and how they shape the look, feel, tone, and rhythm of a brand. You will start to see how every creative choice links back to meaning—choices you can clearly explain to your clients and connect directly to your ShapeDoc and Five Idea Key findings.

An MVB is not about doing less work. It's about doing the right work.

By the end of this section, you'll see how clarity makes the creative process easier, quicker, and far more enjoyable. You'll stop designing in circles and start designing with confidence, because everything you make will have purpose behind it.

So grab a brew, sharpen your pencil, and let's figure out how to turn ideas into brands that actually work for our clients in the real world.

Never
Trust
with a
PORTLAND
AUG
6

Chapter Twenty-One –

WHAT AN MVB REALLY IS

(AND WHY IT MATTERS)

You've probably had a client who comes to you full of excitement, brimming with energy, waving around a half-finished idea and a long list of things they think they need: a logo, a website, an animation, and, in some cases, packaging.

Before you've even had a chance to ask *why* their idea exists, you're knee-deep in a production plan for a brand that hasn't proven whether anyone actually wants what it's selling. You tell yourself it's fine . . . it's work, it's progress, it's what clients expect . . . but somewhere deep down you know it's not right. You're building for the sake of building.

> **THAT'S NOT BRANDING... THAT'S PANIC BRANDING.**

And that's exactly where the idea of an MVB comes in.

Most designers, me included, grew up idolising the big brands. The dream projects, the glossy systems, the ones with endless budgets and huge teams behind them.

Somewhere along the way, we started believing that every brand should look like *that* from day one.

But big-brand thinking only works when you already have all the stuff that makes it possible: things like the audience, the traction, the infrastructure, and the money to back it all up.

Most of the people we work with aren't there yet, and that's okay. When a business is just starting out, it doesn't need a thousand design assets or a fully built-out system.

What it really needs is a clear, confident way to show up in the world and test whether the idea actually works.

"THERE ISN'T
A LOGO IN THE WORLD
THAT WILL SAVE
A SH*T IDEA."

The MVB mindset asks different questions. Not "What can we design?" but "What does this brand actually need *right now* to exist with confidence?"

It's not about cutting corners . . . it's about cutting out the noise. Instead of trying to design everything at once, you're designing just enough: the essential parts that tell the story, hold meaning, and allow the brand to move forward.

The truth is, most early brands don't fail because they look bad. They fail because they build too much too soon. We all remember Saf's story from chapter 15. They pour time and money into elaborate systems, packaging, and websites before they've even tested whether anyone cares.

The founder ends up focusing on how it looks instead of what it actually stands for. When that happens, the brand becomes more performance than progress, an illusion of movement rather than real proof of value. It's a trap that's easy to fall into when the Rush starts taking over. Your role as a designer isn't to build the theatre . . . it's to build the stage. The MVB gives a founder just enough to step on stage, say who they are, and see how the crowd reacts. With a bit of luck, they'll even get a laugh or two.

It's easy to forget that branding at this stage isn't about scale. You're not there to build the empire . . . you're there to help it *stand up*. The MVB gives your clients something real to move with, something they can test and learn from. It's the difference between standing still and starting to build trust. Once the brand has that first bit of momentum, everything else becomes clearer.

When you start working this way, your role changes, too. You stop being the person who makes things and start becoming the person who guides. The MVB mindset turns you into a translator between the absolute chaos in their heads and the clarity that they crave. You're no longer just taking orders; instead, you're helping clients prioritise, slow down, and focus on what really matters. You become the calm voice reminding them that "not now" doesn't mean "never."

That's how you build trust, and that's how reputation sticks. Clients begin to see you differently, not as a pair of hands, but as a creative partner—the person who helps them make smarter decisions, not just the prettier ones. And when they grow, you grow with them. They come back for the next version, not because you did everything, but because you did the right things at the right time.

Lincoln tee design

THE BEAUTY OF AN MVB IS THAT IT KEEPS EVERYONE ADAPTABLE.

When you build a full system too early, you end up locking the brand into choices that might not hold up once it's out in the real world. Suddenly, the colour palette feels untouchable, the typography becomes sacred, and the whole thing starts to stiffen before it's even had a chance to live. Starting small changes that completely. It keeps the brand flexible, open to testing and learning, and easy to evolve as things take shape. That adaptability is gold for both sides because the client learns faster and you get to keep the creative process flowing.

The best thing is that the MVB is fuelled by the Five Idea Keys. The Red Key brings you back to why the brand exists. The Blue Key reminds you who the brand is for and helps you understand your audience. The Green Key shows you where the brand belongs and gives you the context. The Yellow Key defines how the brand behaves and shapes its character. And the Black Key focuses on what the brand offers and why it matters. When you've got those five things nailed, the creative decisions almost make themselves. You know what to design and, more importantly, what not to.

This mindset hasn't just changed how I approach client work; it's become the mindset I use for my own ideas, too. My educational resources didn't begin as something designed for humans who want to start something, shape their ideas, and learn how to build their reputation. They actually started much smaller. It began as free content, which turned into conversations. Those conversations became a simple workshops and courses, which then grew into a twelve-week cohort called The Purple Cloak Crew. From there it evolved again into an idea for a conference called Up the Anty (which never actually happened). After that it shifted once more, first becoming The MBJ Hotel as a talk at Canva Create, and later turning into a small private group for some close design friends. Over the course of about eighteen months, it slowly evolved into what it is today. Every step of that journey was about validation, listening, and shaping. I wanted to make sure it was genuinely useful, and filled with the kinds of lessons and tools that creative people actually needed and could put into action.

An MVB isn't a budget version of branding. It's not a shortcut or a half measure. It's an approach built on focus, restraint, and clarity. It recognises that early-stage brands don't need everything . . . they just need enough to move. It's a shift from designing for completion to designing for traction. And when you think like that, your work gets lighter, faster, and more effective.

Once you start working this way, you'll see it everywhere. You'll notice when brands have been over-designed. You'll spot when clients are hiding behind assets instead of leading with meaning. And you'll realise how powerful it is to start small, stay curious, and grow with intention.

The MVB mindset changes everything. It helps you work smarter, build stronger relationships, and get brands moving with more focus and confidence. More than anything, it reminds you that great design is not measured by how much you make, but by how much meaning you create. That is what this is all about: not doing less, not doing half, but doing the right work.

Chapter Twenty-Two –

FROM KEYS TO BUILDING BLOCKS

So, you've taken the time to ask better questions, uncover meaning, and listen to what really sits beneath the surface of an idea. You've found the Spark, the Person, the Place, the Energy, and the Offer. That work is the glorious foundation for everything else. It's what separates the brands that rush straight into design from those that build something with real purpose.

Now, we move from Discover to Design. This is where the Five Idea Keys start to come to life. They stop being ideas written on a page and begin shaping how the brand looks, feels, and communicates.

Each key plays a natural role in the creative process. When you learn how to read them and apply them, they begin to give form and logic to your work. They take what once felt like instinct and turn it into intention. That is the shift that changes everything. You are no longer designing based on what simply looks good, and you can trace every colour, type choice, and layout back to an idea that actually matters.

When you can do that, it becomes much easier to sell your creative direction to your clients. You are not just showing them what you made; you are showing them why it makes sense.

THE RED KEY: SPARK

Story and Origin

The Red Key pulls you back to the story. It reminds you why the idea exists and what emotion sits behind it. That shapes how the brand communicates. A brand born from frustration will naturally feel bolder and more defiant. A brand born from care will feel calmer and more considered. You start to sense what tone fits and what doesn't.

THE BLUE KEY: PERSON

Tone and Connection

The Blue Key centres you on the person you are designing for. It reminds you that your work is there to connect, not just to impress a load of randoms. Once you are clear on who it is for, you start to make choices that feel right for them. The words, colours, and visuals all begin to match their world. Design stops being about style and starts being about understanding.

THE GREEN KEY: PLACE

Position and Contrast

The Green Key helps you see where the brand lives and what else exists around it. This context directs how far you push things. Sometimes the right move is to blend in, and other times it is to completely stand apart. The Green Key gives you that awareness. You start noticing how design choices either echo or challenge the world they sit within.

THE YELLOW KEY: ENERGY

Feeling and Flow

The Yellow Key shapes the brand's energy. It sets the pace and the mood. Some ideas move fast and loud, while others breathe a little slower and softer. This key helps you translate that energy into a visual direction. It guides how colour, form, and motion come together to express personality before a single word is read. It can also influence voice and word choice, helping the brand sound the way it feels.

THE BLACK KEY: OFFER

Structure and Clarity

The Black Key grounds everything. It reminds you what the brand is offering and what people need to understand first. It directs hierarchy, layout, and focus. It ensures every design has a clear purpose and a simple path for the viewer to follow. When this key is in place, your work feels not only creative but also functional.

5 The Five Idea Keys

Together, these keys stop you from guessing. They give every choice a reason. When you design this way, your work gains clarity and confidence. You can explain your instincts and show clients how your creative direction connects back to strategy. Nothing is random anymore. Every decision has meaning, and that meaning becomes the foundation of great design. Every choice supports the story . . . pretty damn cool, huh?

- **Red shapes story and origin:** It informs concept and creative direction.
- **Blue shapes tone:** It influences voice, personality, and empathy.
- **Green shapes context:** It defines contrast and positioning.
- **Yellow shapes character:** It brings emotion and rhythm.
- **Black shapes clarity:** It organises information and drives action.

In the next chapter, we'll explore how certain keys help us shape the visual direction of a brand, how they remove decision fatigue from the process, and how they make every choice feel simple.

Chapter Twenty-Three –

MAKING VISUAL DECISIONS SIMPLE

Now, we get to the good bit: making it all visual. You know by now that design isn't decoration; it's translation. Every colour, line, and layout choice should be reacting to what the brand stands for. When you think like that, you stop getting stuck in your head. You stop chasing colour trends and adding unnecessary noise, and you realise your job isn't to add more; it's to reveal what truly matters.

Here's a simple rule to keep in mind. Not every key needs to show up in the visuals, but the ones that do should guide your decisions. The keys are filters, not a checklist you have to tick off. The Red Key might influence the logo idea. The Blue Key might shape the tone or type choices. The Yellow Key might set the overall mood and personality of the design. The Green Key keeps everything connected to the world it belongs in, and the Black Key brings structure and clarity to it all.

When you start to see design through that lens, the distractions fade away. You don't need to explore endless options just to see what feels right. You can make choices faster and with more confidence because they come from meaning, not guesswork. Keep your own design process; just use the keys as your brief. The keys are there to guide your decisions, not to limit how many concepts or revisions you create. That part is completely up to you, my friend. You get to design your own way.

Two of the keys usually shape the visuals more than the others for me: the Spark and the Energy.

The Spark is where the idea begins. It reminds you what story you are telling and what feeling sits underneath it. If the Spark came from frustration, the design might feel sharp and full of contrast. If it came from care or curiosity, it might feel softer, with rounder shapes and a more natural flow.

Energy gives a brand its personality. Some brands move fast; others take their time. That feeling shapes everything: the type, the spacing, the colours, even how the design moves. You can usually feel it when it works. Fast brands often use bold type, strong contrasts, and vibrant colours. Slower brands breathe through softer tones, wider spacing, and gentle transitions.

Think about a brand with bold, high energy—like a streetwear label. The design moves fast. The typography is tight and punchy. The palette hits hard with contrast. Everything feels alive and confident.

Now, imagine a brand with calm, low energy—maybe a wellness coach. The design slows down. The typography opens up. The colours soften. There is more air, more space, more breathing room.

Both feel right because they express their individual energy truthfully.

While the Red and Yellow Keys set the tone, the others keep things balanced. The Person keeps you focused on who you are designing for and reminds you to make things clear and easy for them to understand. The Place helps you position the brand visually in its world and decide how it fits or stands out. The Offer keeps everything practical. It shapes hierarchy, calls to action, and visual flow so the design works as well as it looks. Together, these keys help you see the brand as a connected system, not just a collection of parts.

One of the hardest parts of design is knowing what not to do. You want clients to come to you for your taste and judgment as much as your creativity. When you have a strong foundation, you do not need to design everything at once. You only need to design what matters for now: the MVB. The rest can grow later once the idea is tested and proven. Restraint is not a lack of creativity; I actually believe it's proof of confidence. It is saying, "This is enough for now, and I know why."

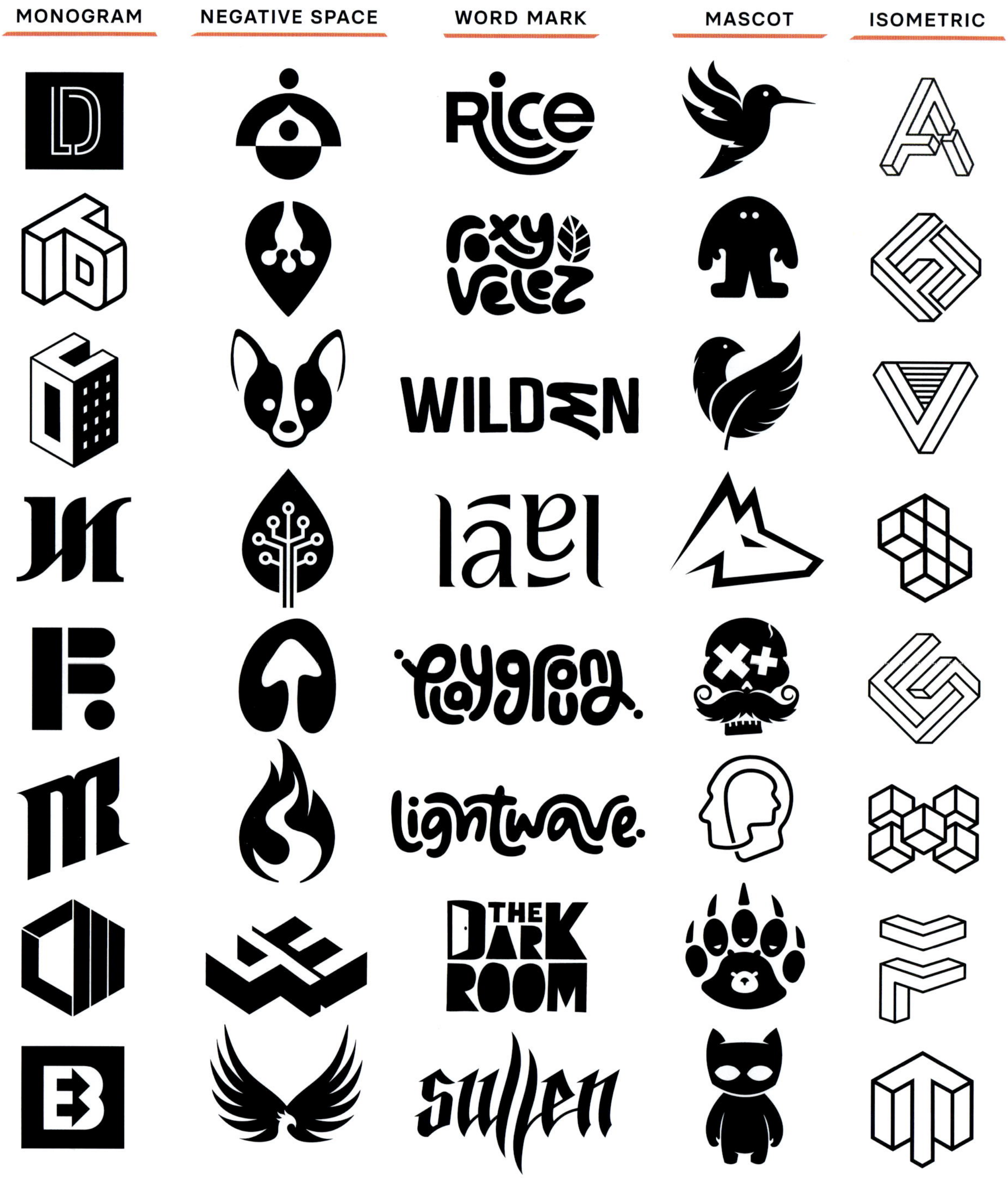
MONOGRAM
NEGATIVE SPACE
WORD MARK
MASCOT
ISOMETRIC

THE BEST DESIGNERS ARE OFTEN THE MOST DISCIPLINED ONES. THEY KNOW WHEN TO STOP.

There will always be moments in the design process where instinct leads first; that is normal. We are emotional, sassy, creative humans after all. The goal is not to remove intuition; it is to back it up with proper reasoning. When something feels right, pause for a second and ask yourself why. Which key does it connect to? What does it express? How does it link to the idea? That reflection is what makes your instincts powerful.

The moment you start designing with meaning, everything shifts. You stop thinking only about how something looks and start thinking about what it represents. That is where your reputation grows, when clients see that you care about the bigger picture, not just the portfolio piece. You become known for your discernment, your ideas, and your ability to make things feel right for a reason.

In the next chapter, we will take this thinking further and look at how to give the idea a voice, because a brand is more than how it looks; it is how it speaks. We will explore how to shape language and tone that match the design, helping your clients sound as confident and intentional as they now look.

Chapter Twenty-Four –

FINDING YOUR VOICE AND LANGUAGE

For a long time, I thought design was all about visuals. The logo, the colours, the shapes, the layout . . . that was my world and I was never going to budge from it. I obsessed over how things looked and how they fit together on the page. But I completely underestimated the tribal power of tone, voice, and proper messaging.

It took me years to realise that people don't just connect to what they see, they connect to how something sounds. The words, the rhythm, and the honesty behind them are what build belonging. You can have the best-looking brand in the world, but people will ultimately get bored of visuals. They are easier to copy, easier to imitate, and without a heartbeat behind them, they fade pretty fast.

The way you speak, the words you choose, and the stories you tell—that is what creates real connection.

And there is actually a bit of science to back that up. Our brains process visuals in a flash, almost instantly, but unless those visuals are tied to story or sound, they disappear just as quickly. Language works completely differently. It fires up the parts of the brain linked to memory, emotion, and even movement. When someone hears words that feel honest or familiar, their brain starts to mirror yours. Scientists call it neural coupling, but really it just means they are feeling what you feel. That's why words linger in people's minds long after an image disappears.

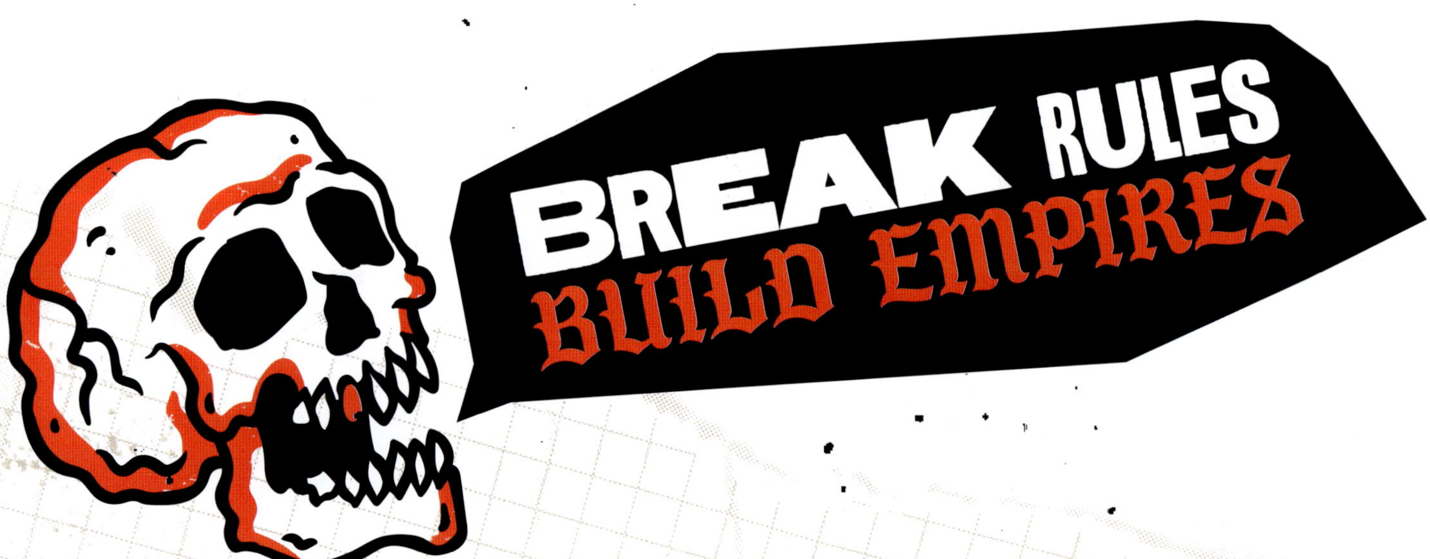

VISUALS GRAB ATTENTION. WORDS BUILD ATTACHMENT.

That's why the title of this book is *No Bullsh*t Branding*. It's not a slogan: It's a statement. It sets the tone before you read a single word. That's my voice. Real, direct, human, a little spicy, but always grounded in honesty. It's the same tone I use in my newsletters, in workshops, and when I speak on stage. It's not for everyone, and that's the point. Your tone attracts your people.

The way I talk has become part of my reputation. The title makes sense to the people who know me, support me, and have followed my journey. They understand the intent behind it, and it feels familiar. I don't swear to be cool . . . trust me, I go hiking and I'm in bed by half eight most nights. It's just the way I speak when I'm passionate about the work and the things I care about.

Depending on where I show up, I turn the dial up or down. I swear a little less here because the publishers asked me to, a bit more when I'm hanging out in my community, and never when I'm teaching kids at their schools. But the energy doesn't change. It's still me, just adjusted for the room I am in.

Finding the right voice always starts with empathy. You're not writing for yourself; you're writing for someone else. It's about helping them feel seen and understood. The best tone doesn't come from trying to sound smart—it comes from caring about who's listening.

The Blue Key, which is all about the Person, helps you remember who you're actually talking to. What kind of world do they live in? How do they speak? What kind of language makes them feel understood? When you know that, it becomes a lot easier to write in a way that feels real. If your audience talks in a natural, human way, your brand should match that.

Then, there's the Yellow Key, the Energy. Every idea carries a certain feeling. Some have more intensity and attitude; others feel more reserved and steady. That energy should come through in how you write. If the idea is bold, let the words be confident. If the idea is more thoughtful, let the words feel slower and more open. The way you write should match the feeling of the brand.

I know what you might be thinking: "I'm not a writer." But I promise, you don't need to be. You already work with flow, space, and people's feelings every day. Writing works the same way. You can tell when something reads right, just like you can tell when a layout doesn't feel right. It's not about being good with words; it's about trusting your creative instincts and, more importantly, knowing what doesn't work for a brand. Remember the inversion process from earlier in the book.

When visuals and voice align, trust builds fast. Gentle design needs language that feels open and grounded. Expressive design needs words that carry strength and confidence. If your visuals are full of play, let your words move with the same energy. If your design speaks softly, don't let the copy shout at the reader, like my title does. It's about keeping things in sync. When both sides work together, the brand feels effortless.

Verbal identity isn't about lists of adjectives or endless brand documents. It's about showing up the same way everywhere. When you speak with consistency, people begin to trust the tone as much as the message. That's how a voice becomes a part of a brand's reputation.

The Offer—the Black Key—helps you structure what you say. Think of it like layout logic: Something always leads, something supports. The headline carries the emotion, the subtext gives clarity, the call to action drives movement. Design and writing follow the same rhythm of meaning.

You don't need to rewrite every line your client gives you or write all the copy for them. That's not the MVB way. Your job is to help them find clarity, not to do their marketing homework. Once you've shaped the Offer Stack and the Offer Line, you already have the language that can grow into their messaging. It gives you the raw material for headlines, taglines, and tone of voice. Check out the following example.

Example: Coffee Shop

Take our coffee shop example from earlier.

Offer Line
We help people slow down and reconnect by serving great coffee in calm, intentional spaces so they can leave feeling grounded and ready for the day.

Website Header
Coffee. Connection. Calm.

Intro Paragraph
Life moves fast. Our cafés are designed to help you slow down. Every cup, every pastry, every smile . . . all made to give you a moment of calm in your day.

Social Bio Example
Helping people slow down, one coffee at a time.

This is how the Offer Line grows from a simple exercise into the foundation of your client's MVB. It helps shape their voice, guides the tone of their words, and gives them something real and confident to say when they talk about what they do.

When you start treating words as part of your design tool kit, everything gets clearer. You'll begin to notice when something sounds off before you even look at the page. You'll catch when a layout feels wrong because the language doesn't flow. You'll see that shaping words is just another way of shaping meaning.

The way you speak becomes part of your reputation. It shows people what you stand for and what they can expect from you. It's how trust begins to form, often before anyone has seen your work. You don't need to be a writer; you just need to care about how things sound and what they make people feel.

Good designers don't just make brands look right. They make them feel right. And that feeling always starts with the words you choose.

Chapter Twenty-Five –

POSITIONING YOURSELF IN THE WILD

Sasha Strauss

There's a company called Loom—you might have even used it. It's a simple little tool that lets you record your screen and share quick videos. When they first launched, their messaging was clean and clear, but completely forgettable. "Record your screen. Share instantly." It did the job, but it didn't hit you anywhere that mattered. It was just another piece of tech for people who already had too much tech.

The team eventually realised people weren't using Loom because they wanted to record their screens. They were using it because they were sick of meetings. They were tired of the endless back-and-forth, the wasted hours on calls that could have been explained in sixty seconds. Loom wasn't a tool anymore. It was a middle finger to calendar chaos.

So, Loom made one simple change. They shifted their message from what it did to why it mattered. They started saying, "No more meetings."

That single line changed everything. The product didn't change, the features didn't change, but the meaning completely did. Suddenly Loom wasn't just another screen recorder you used for quick demos. It represented freedom, a way out of endless Zoom calls and calendar overload. They hadn't just tweaked their marketing; they'd reshaped how people felt about them. They'd repositioned their reputation.

And the numbers back it up. By the time they were acquired by Atlassian, Loom had more than 25 million users and people were recording around 5 million videos every month. Inside Atlassian, Loom helped save over 3.75 million minutes of meeting time, the equivalent of more than 375,000 meetings.

Did the line "No more meetings" cause all that growth? Probably not by itself. But it changed the story people told themselves about the product. It sharpened their edge. It gave people a shorthand, a belief, that this was something bigger than a screen recorder. That's what smart positioning does. It doesn't just explain what something is—it changes what people believe it means.

You might remember the quote from Sasha Strauss back in chapter 9:

IF YOU DON'T POSITION YOURSELF, YOU WILL BE POSITIONED.

That line sits right at the heart of what we do as designers. Because if you don't define where something belongs, the world will happily decide for you.

That's the brutal truth of branding. Most people don't see the full picture. They'll never read the strategy deck, or sit through your workshop, or understand the emotional logic behind your logo choices. They'll see one message, one product, one passing moment, and they'll make up their own story.

That's perception.

Your job as a designer is to shape that perception. To give people the right clues and the right signals so the story they build in their head actually lines up with the truth behind the idea.

Most people will never see all the evidence, the process, the care, or the meaning behind what has been built, so your work has to act as the proof. Every visual choice, every word, every behaviour becomes a small piece of evidence that tells the right story. That is what positioning really is. It is not about being louder or trendier or cleverer. It is about giving your clients the best chance to put their reputation in the right place and back it up with visible proof that they belong there.

And if this still feels like a lot, honestly, don't worry about it. You're not supposed to have it all figured out yet. None of us do at the start. The more you design, the more you build your own reputation, the more all of this starts to click into place. I've got twenty-odd years of this stuff buzzing around my head, so don't compare where you are now to that. Positioning stops feeling like theory the more you do it. It becomes instinct. You start to see patterns faster, read the room easier, and connect your design decisions to what the brand actually stands for.

Lincoln crew in the wild

THE IMPORTANCE OF EVIDENCE

Random aligned thought incoming. I really believe evidence is going to matter more than ever. The internet is filling up with nonhuman slop—things that look the part but have no heart or truth behind them. When that happens, **perception might get attention, but evidence earns trust—and trust is what lasts.** The brands that can *show* what they stand for, not just *say* it, will win. **Perception gets attention. Evidence earns trust—and trust is what compounds.**

I think the next big shift in branding won't be about making more content. It'll be about building what I call "Evidence Engines"—systems that prove credibility rather than just claim it. Brands need credibility strategies, not content strategies.

This is where the Green Key comes back to life. The Green Key isn't just about geography. It's about Place in the wider sense of context. Where does this idea live? What world is it stepping into? What are the rules of that world, and where's the opportunity to bend them?

Before you design anything, you have to know where you are designing for. Is it something people will pick up on a shelf, scroll past on a feed, or experience in person? Is it living in this country, another culture, or across the world? The environment changes everything, the tone, the visuals, the feeling. Who's already there? What's everyone saying? What do they look like? What are they missing? When you understand that, you start seeing the patterns. You start seeing what has been overused, what has been done to death, and where the gaps are.

Once you know where the idea sits, every design choice becomes easier. Colour, type, tone, texture: they all start to align. You're not designing to impress. You're designing to fit in the right place, in the right way, for the right people. You're designing evidence of difference.

And this is where the keys start to shape positioning on their own. The **Red Key** anchors the reason the brand exists, which sets the foundation for what it should be known for. The **Blue Key** defines who the brand is speaking to, which decides the language, tone, and cultural space it needs to show up in. The **Green Key** reveals the environment and competitive landscape, helping you understand the norms you are reacting to. The **Yellow Key** adds energy and personality, showing how the brand moves and behaves within that landscape.

When you bring those pieces together, positioning stops being guesswork. You can see where the idea belongs, what space it can own, and how to express that difference with confidence. The keys give you the full picture—purpose, audience, environment, and behaviour—everything you need to decide exactly where the brand should live and how it should stand apart.

As a designer, this is the lens that will help you package up your offers, too. The better you get at reading these layers and positioning ideas, the easier it becomes to guide clients through it. You stop selling "design" and start delivering understanding. You help people make sense of where their brand belongs, what makes it different, and how to show that difference clearly.

Now, onward to "packaging the offer."

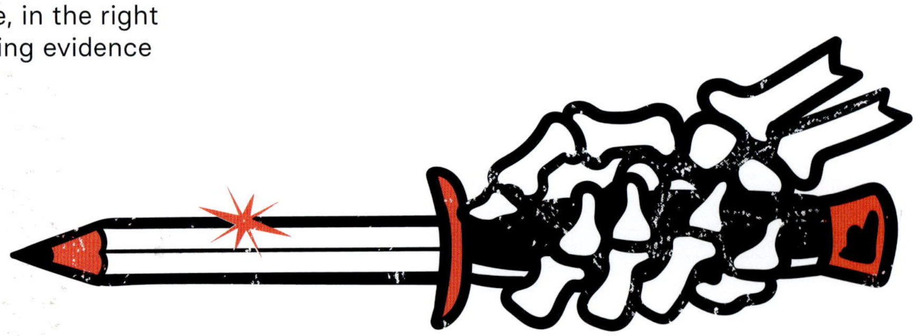

A TRUE USP

As designers, we often hear people talk about a USP—a unique selling point. It's one of those phrases that gets mentioned a lot but rarely explained in a way that actually helps. So, I thought I'd have a go at defining a simple framework that makes it easier to grasp and easier to explain.

At some point, every designer gets asked, *"So what makes you different?"*

That's what a USP helps you answer. When it's clear, people instantly understand who you're for and why you're right for them. It gives your work focus and helps others see its value without you having to oversell it.

A true USP isn't just a catchy line. It's the heart of what makes you different and why that difference matters. When you can say it clearly, you stop sounding like just another designer and start sounding like a brand.

> **If you can answer these four things,
> you've already got the makings of a strong USP:**
>
> 1. **Who it's for:** The specific people you're here to help
> 2. **The problem:** The pain or need you solve
> 3. **Why you're different:** Your unique way of approaching it
> 4. **The outcome:** What people walk away with

Here's a real example, built around the ideas in this book:

* **Who it's for:** Humans with raw ideas, but no real brand.
* **The problem:** I provide a simple framework (the Five Idea Keys) that helps shape those ideas into something they can actually launch.
* **Why I'm different :** I stand out through my mix of punk energy and proven credibility (Lincoln, Canva, Affinity), and keeping things clear, human, and accessible . . . even on smaller budgets.
* **The outcome:** People walk away with a *Minimum Viable Brand* they can sell and grow with confidence.

That's the power of a clear USP.
It speaks for you . . . even when you're not in the room.

NO BULLSH*T BRANDING

Chapter Twenty-Six –

PACKAGE THE OFFER

Right now it's time to turn that internal clarity into something the world can actually see, understand, and buy.

In the Black Key, you built the Offer from the inside out. You explored what the brand believes in, what it gives, and what people walk away with. That gave it backbone. Now, it's time to flip it.

You're moving from the inside of the brand to the outside, from meaning to message, from theory to proof. This is the point where a brand stops being an idea and starts becoming something people can connect with.

Most designers stop just before this. Not because they're lazy or wrong, but because that's how the industry trained us: Make it look great, hand it over, move on. And early in your career, that makes sense. You're proving your craft. But over time, you realise the truth. If clients can't explain or use what you've made, the brand never really takes off.

I learned that the hard way. I'd hand over beautiful systems that ticked every box, but when clients tried to launch, they got stuck. They had all the ingredients but no recipe. That's when it clicked for me. Design isn't finished when it looks good; it's finished when it works, when it helps people understand what the business offers and gives the client the confidence to share it.

That's what this next stage is about. You've already shaped the brand's idea. Now, you help it speak. You don't need more theory, just a clear, practical way to show what the brand gives and who it's for.

I call it the Packaged Pathway, or simply, the 3 Ps. It's the simplest way to take everything you've built inside the brand and turn it into something real and usable. It's by no means a new concept and there are plenty of variations out there, but its role is always the same: focus.

Every offer, no matter the size or type, comes down to three parts:

> **1. A Person**
> **2. With a Problem**
> **3. Taken on a Path**

Those three elements work everywhere. The Person tells you who it's for. The Problem gives it purpose. The Path shows how you'll move them from where they are to where they want to be.

When I talk about packaging the offer, I'm not talking theory. This is something I had to figure out inside my own studio and have since helped other studio owners with, too.

It started with a simple question: How can I help founders turn their raw ideas into real brands? That question shaped everything we do. Working through the MVB mindset, I began turning that idea into something tangible, a structured offer that made sense of the work we'd been doing for years.

It grew directly out of my own keys.

The *Person* I wanted to help was clear: founders with ideas, energy, and ambition.

The *Problem* they faced was simple: They were embarrassed by what they had and didn't know how to build trust or grow something that felt right.

And the *Path* was something I'd refined over years of practice: a guided process called Discovery, Design, and Delivery (DDD). It's how we move people from confusion to clarity, from idea to identity, from hesitation to momentum.

It's not about selling brand design or handing over a logo package. Those things are outcomes. What I'm really selling is a pathway that helps a real person go through a real transformation.

That's something every designer should think about for their clients, not as another service to add, but as a mindset.

When you're in client mode, look beyond the visuals and help the client see what they're really offering. Even a short conversation about their offer can completely change how you design. It gives you context and makes sure every asset supports something meaningful.

And when you switch into solo mode, this thinking becomes even more valuable. You need your own offer, too, something clear and specific that speaks to a real person with a real problem. When you know that, marketing stops feeling like guesswork. You know who you're talking to, what to say, and how to show the value of what you do.

PACKAGE THE OFFER

Whether you're working for clients or for yourself, this mindset keeps you grounded. Every strong brand, and every strong designer, starts with clarity about what's being offered and why it matters.

And here's the best part. The DDD process doesn't just help me deliver the work—it helps me sell it. When I'm on calls with potential clients, I can walk them through what happens in each step, why it matters, and how the stages connect to create real results. It gives me confidence because I'm not just selling design; I'm guiding them through a process that makes sense. And it gives them confidence because they can see the value of every step before we even begin.

That's the power of a well-packaged offer. It doesn't just serve the client, it strengthens you, too.

Every brand's MVB will look different because every business is different. The café might need packaging and a menu. The gym might need a one-page site and signage. The law firm might need a few key documents to explain what they do. Your offer should flex around the world your client lives in.

The 3 Ps give you a framework to guide those decisions without ever boxing you in. They help you think clearly and design intentionally while keeping the output personal and practical.

When you do this right, everything clicks. Clients speak with confidence. They can explain what they do and why it matters. The visuals and the words work together, and the brand feels whole, not because it's polished, but because it's honest.

That's what builds trust. That's what people talk about. They don't rave about colour palettes or fonts. They talk about clarity. They tell others that you helped them figure out what they were really offering and gave them something they could use straight away.

That's what spreads. That's how your reputation grows.

Packaging the offer is where meaning turns into momentum. It's where everything inside the MVB starts to come alive in the real world. And while every offer will look different, the principle stays the same.

> **One Person.**
> **One Problem.**
> **One Path.**

The 3 Ps.

Simple, clear, and flexible enough to shape any brand you'll ever build.

Now, it's time to pull it all together. The next step is turning that offer, and everything you've created so far, into a usable MVB tool kit your client can actually put to work.

BE A GOOD HUMAN
BE A FORCE FOR GOOD
Canva
MAKE Complex things SIMPLE
Canva
BE A FORCE FOR GOOD
Canva
SET CRAZY BIG GOALS AND MAKE THEM HAPPEN
SET CRAZY Big Goals AND MAKE THEM HAPPEN
Canva
PURSUE EXCELLENCE
Canva
BE A GOOD HUMAN
EMPOWER Canva OTHERS
Canva
BE A GOOD HUMAN
Canva
BE A Good HUMAN
Canva
MAKE Complex things SIMPLE
BE A GOOD HUMAN
Empower OTHERS
SET CRAZY Big Goals AND MAKE THEM HAPPEN
Canva
BE A FORCE FOR GOOD
EMPOWER OTHERS
Canva
EMPOWER OTHERS
Canva
BE A GOOD HUMAN Estd 2013
SET CRAZY BIG GOALS AND MAKE THEM HAPPEN
BE A GOOD HUMAN
Canva
BE A Good HUMAN
Canva
MAKE Complex things SIMPLE
Canva
BE A FORCE FOR GOOD
Canva
BE A FORCE FOR GOOD
Empower OTHERS
Canva
EMPOWER Canva OTHERS

Chapter Twenty-Seven –

ASSEMBLE YOUR MVB KIT

The MVB is not a half brand. It's not an unfinished project or a cheaper version of the real thing. It's built for something completely different. It's built for movement. It's built to help ideas get out into the world and find their feet before anyone goes all in.

Most designers have been taught that a brand isn't a brand until every detail is polished and perfectly packaged. The MVB flips that idea on its head. It's not about showing how much you can do. It's about doing just enough to get a client started.

If somebody comes to you with a big budget, a clear direction, and the resources to go deep, you should absolutely build the full thing. That's what they're ready for. The MVB isn't a replacement for that. It's an option for the people who aren't there yet.

In every designer's career, there will be clients who come to you at the very beginning. They've got an idea, a small budget, and a lot of energy. They believe in what they're building, but have no idea where to start. That's where the MVB comes in. It gives them a way to begin with focus and intention instead of panic and guesswork. It's a starter brand, not a shortcut.

I've been in this industry for twenty years and I still meet people like that all the time—people with brilliant ideas and no road map. They don't need a full identity system. They just need a small, clear set of tools to help them test, share, and shape their idea in the real world. The MVB gives you a way to help them do exactly that.

What I love about this approach is that it gives designers flexibility. You don't have to turn people away just because they can't afford a big project. You can meet them where they are. You can build something small and intentional that still makes a real difference. And if they grow, you grow with them. The MVB becomes the start of a long relationship, not a one-off job.

It also changes how you think about your own work. Even when I'm working on larger projects, the MVB mindset is always in the background. It reminds me to stay focused on what the brand actually needs right now, not just what I'd like to create for it. It helps me strip away the unnecessary and build brands that move with purpose.

So, what does an MVB kit actually look like? It's simple. Everything in the kit should be something the client can actually use—things that help them test their idea, share their story, and show up consistently. Nothing in there should exist just to fill space.

Here's what a typical kit might include:

MVB KIT ESSENTIALS

* **A simple logo** that works everywhere: Shaped by the *Red Key* (Spark) and *Yellow Key* (Energy)

* **A colour palette** with no more than three purposeful colours: Guided by the *Yellow Key* (Energy) and *Green Key* (Place)

* **A type system** with two or three fonts (one for headers, one for highlights, one for copy): Connected to the *Blue Key* (Person) and *Yellow Key* (Energy)

* **A short messaging guide** to help the brand speak clearly and consistently: Built from the *Red*, *Blue*, and *Black Keys* (Spark, Person, Offer)

* **A handful of offer visuals or mock-ups** that show the product or service in action: Tied to the *Black Key* (Offer) and *Green Key* (Place)

* **One main launch platform:** A single-page website, a PDF, or a social profile, anchored by the *Black Key* and *Green Key*

* **A folder of usable assets,** labelled and easy to find: Linked to *all the keys*

* **A few simple rules or notes** explaining how to use it all: Also linked to *all the keys*

That's the foundation. After that, things start to flex. Some clients might need packaging mock-ups. Some might need social templates, business cards, or pitch slides. The point is that every kit should be built around the client's stage and needs. You use your judgment, guided by the brand's values and goals, to decide what really belongs.

When you present this kind of work, help clients understand what they're getting. You're not selling them less. You're helping them start smart. Tell them it's not unfinished, it's evolving. It's designed to grow as they learn more about their offer and audience.

Over time, the MVB can become an offer inside your own studio—a smaller package you can provide to early-stage founders or creators who need clarity fast. It's the kind of offer that opens doors to new relationships and lets you work with people who might otherwise have been out of reach. It gives you a way to make an impact earlier in someone's journey.

The best part is that the MVB mindset naturally leads to better design decisions everywhere else. It teaches restraint. It teaches focus. It reminds you that the job isn't to design for the sake of designing.

So, when you're assembling an MVB kit, think small, but think smart. Build something real, usable, and clear. Something that gives your client a way to start, to show up, and to learn on the fly. That's all it needs to do. Get them out into the real world, testing their ideas with real people. That's what sets them up for success.

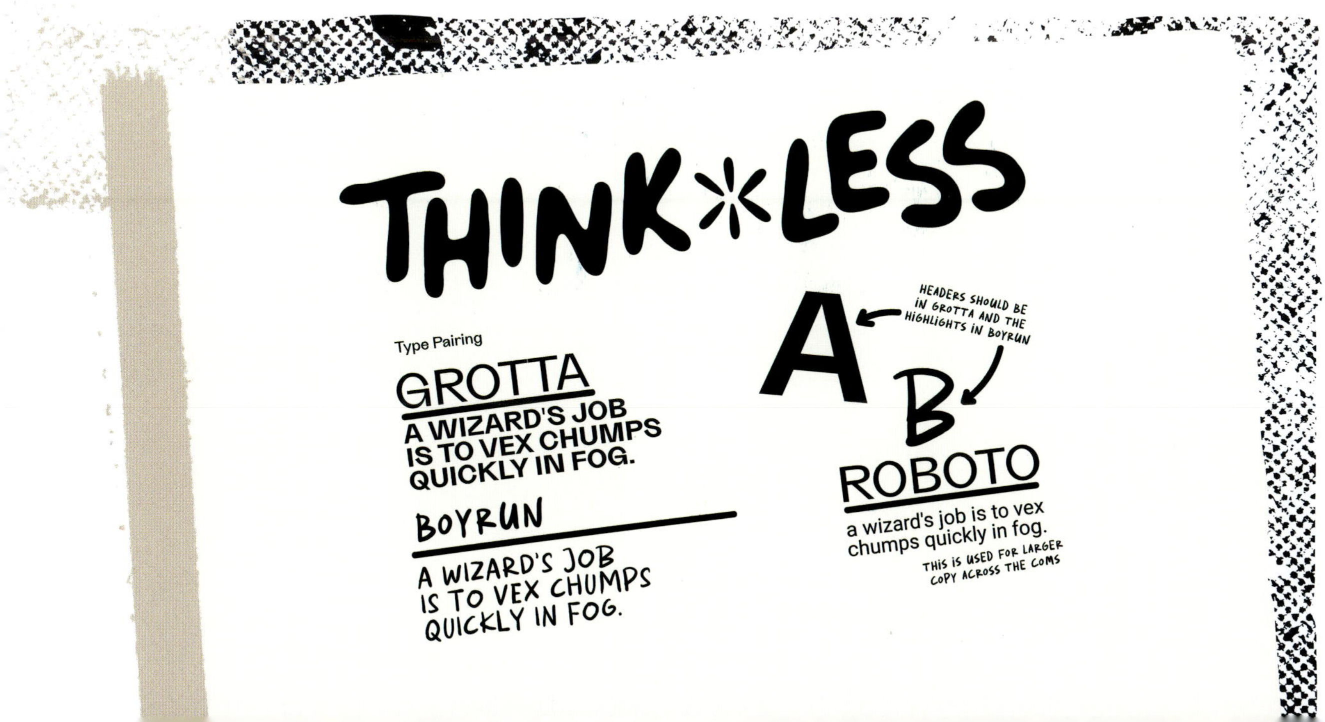

SECTION FIVE

LAUNCH WITHOUT PANIC

Nice one, mate. You've made it to section five. You have the patience of a saint.

This is the part that's really going to help your clients, but truthfully, it's going to help you, too. You now understand how the Five Idea Keys work and how they help shape an idea into something clear and usable. You've also got a good sense of what an MVB is and who it's for. Now, it's time to explore what happens next and how to get that idea out into the world without losing your head in the process.

The launch is where things usually start to go sideways. This is where panic branding loves to sneak back in. Clients hit "Publish" and suddenly feel like they need to be everywhere, post everything, and move at the speed of the internet. Before long, all that calm, intentional thinking disappears under the rush.

Your job now is to help them launch without panic. To slow things down, remove the rush from their mindset, and guide them toward building trust one small, real moment at a time.

Content strategy was built for the attention economy. Credibility strategy was built for the evidence economy.

There's already so much noise and nonsense out there that the brands who will truly thrive are the ones proving things in the real world. Real results. Real people. Real progress.

That's what this section is all about. We're shifting from content to credibility, from chasing likes to earning trust. And I've got some fun, practical stuff to share that will help you and your clients build belief, proof, and belonging that actually lasts.

Section five is the story of how an idea earns belief—from the first stranger to a trusted reputation.

Let's crack on.

Chapter Twenty-Eight –

THE FIRST STRANGER

Alright mate, this is where things start to get properly exciting—or at least, I get properly excited about this stuff, but I'm weird.

Truth bomb alert: A brand doesn't really begin until it meets the world.

You can do all the thinking, shaping, and planning you like, but until someone who has never heard of it sees it, reacts to it, and decides it's worth their time, it's still just an idea. The moment it leaves the safety of the studio, the screen, or the client's head—that's when it becomes something truly real, and that can be frightening.

There's actually a bit of psychology behind why that moment feels so uncomfortable. When something only exists in our heads, it's perfect. It can't be questioned, rejected, or misunderstood. It lives in what psychologists call the *comfort zone*, where imagination is safe and failure doesn't exist. The second you let it out into the world, you introduce risk. You invite feedback, judgment, and, sometimes, silence. Our brains are wired to avoid that kind of uncertainty because it triggers the same stress responses as physical danger. That's why so many ideas stay hidden in notebooks or on hard drives. We'd rather protect them than see them tested.

But that's also the exact reason the first stranger matters so much. It's the step that breaks that loop. It's the moment where fear turns into data, and data turns into confidence. Once your client sees even one real person respond with curiosity instead of criticism, the fear starts to fade. The idea moves from fragile to functional.

That moment is when the brand earns its first bit of credibility. It's proof that something you've helped build actually connects with another human being. It's no longer theory or strategy. It's evidence. And that evidence comes in the shape of what I like to call the *First Stranger.*

The First Stranger is that person who discovers the brand with fresh eyes. They're not a mate doing you a favour or a relative being polite. They're someone with no reason to care, yet something about the brand makes them stop. Maybe they read a line that clicks. Maybe they see a colour or a symbol that feels right.

TRUTH BOMB ALERT: A BRAND DOESN'T REALLY BEGIN UNTIL IT MEETS THE WORLD.

Maybe they watch a short clip and think, "This is actually for me." Whatever it is, that spark is where it all begins.

The first stranger is the real test. Friends and family are lovely, but their feedback comes wrapped in kindness. Strangers give you truth. If they stick around, it means the work you've done with your client is clear enough and human enough to cut through. That's when the brand takes its first breath in the wild.

It's a huge moment. One stranger might not sound like much, but it's everything. It's the first drop of proof that what's been built makes sense outside of the small circle of people who created it. It's the bridge between imagination and reality, and it's what separates a good idea from a living brand.

Your job as the designer is to help your clients find that first stranger and understand why that moment matters. It's not about reach or popularity at this stage. It's about validation. It's about showing that what they've built has the power to connect with someone new.

The great news is that finding that first stranger isn't as hard or mysterious as it sounds. It's not about shouting louder or spending big. It's about being deliberate and human. The goal isn't to chase attention, it's to invite connection.

Start by helping your client think about who that stranger might be. Ask questions like:

- **Who is one person this could genuinely help?**
- **Where would that person spend their time?**
- **What simple thing could we share that gives them something to react to?**

Here's a tip that always works well. The easiest way to find your first stranger is through someone you already know.

If your client has a friend, family member, or colleague who loves what they're building, get that person to introduce them to someone in their own world who might benefit from it. It's not a cold pitch, but it's not a comfort-zone chat either. It's a warm introduction to the real world.

That first introduction can lead to a conversation, a small sale, or a piece of honest feedback. Whatever happens, it's useful. It gives your client data, direction, and a little burst of belief. It's the first bit of real evidence that what they've built actually works.

When that happens, encourage them to slow down and take it in. What caught the stranger's attention? What confused them? What got them excited? This is where learning begins. Every reaction is valuable, even the awkward ones.

If that stranger becomes a fan, even better. Fans tell stories. They talk about what they've found. They invite new people in. And that's how credibility grows—not in big leaps, but through real human ripples.

Help your clients redefine success around that idea. It's not about going viral. It's about finding proof that the brand works. If one stranger connects, that's success. If one person buys, that's success. If one person says, "I love what you're doing," that's success. Because that means the idea has moved from concept to connection.

This approach takes the panic out of launching. It stops your clients from obsessing over numbers or noise and reminds them that building a brand is a series of small, believable steps. It also takes the pressure off you as the designer. You don't need to hand over a perfect, finished masterpiece. You just need to create something clear enough to earn belief from one person.

THAT'S THE WORK THAT MATTERS.

When your client finds that first stranger, tell them to celebrate it. Tell them to thank the stranger, ask questions, and learn something new. That interaction might seem small, but it's the most honest part of brand building. It's the first moment of truth.

And from there, things start to grow naturally. The next stranger might come from a share, a referral, or a conversation. The story spreads slowly and calmly, and suddenly the brand isn't just being built—it's being believed in.

That's the path we're heading down next. We'll talk about how to attract more of those right people and build a small but mighty group of believers who actually care.

But for now, remember this. The first stranger is where everything starts. One real connection, one genuine response, one small moment of belief. That's the beginning of trust, and good reputations are always built on trust.

MADE BY JAMES
THE HONEST GUIDE TO CREATIVITY AND LOGO DESIGN
NIKE
Creative South '24

Chapter Twenty-Nine –

ATTRACTING THE RIGHT PEOPLE

Alright pal, now that your client has met their First Stranger, it's time to start attracting more of the right kind of people. And I mean the right kind. Not everyone, not anyone, just the ones who actually get it. The ones who believe what the brand stands for. The ones who need what your client offers.

This is where most people lose their heads. They see a glimmer of interest and suddenly convince themselves they need to be everywhere at once. They start posting daily, following trends, launching podcasts, and trying to master every platform going. They think visibility equals success, when really all they're doing is adding more noise to an already noisy world. Trust me, I've been that person.

The truth is, the brands that win aren't the loudest. They're the ones that back up what they say with proof. You've seen this before, in the section opener:

Content strategy was built for the attention economy.
Credibility strategy was built for the evidence economy.

The attention economy rewards speed, frequency, and hype. It's about chasing the next moment of visibility. But the evidence economy rewards honesty, consistency, and trust. It's not about being seen everywhere. It's about being believed somewhere. And belief is what builds belonging. People want to be part of something real, and belonging starts with trust.

That's what we're really doing when we help clients attract people. We're not helping them chase followers or fake hype. We're helping them build belonging through proof. We want to help them earn belief.

The good news is that trust doesn't need to be complicated. It just needs to be consistent. People are tired of being shouted at. They don't want to be sold to in every post. They want to believe. They want to see that what a brand says matches what it does. They want the evidence.

That's where the Evidence Engines come in.

They're simple, repeatable systems that turn everyday actions into trust signals. They quietly prove competence, integrity, and reliability. They're not built to get attention. They're built to deserve it.

If you want to dive deeper, you can find loads of examples and templates by scanning the QR code on page 113. But let's start with the basics right here.

Before we jump in, a quick note. The examples I'm sharing for each engine are written with designers and small studios in mind. That's our world. But the same principles apply to your clients, too. As you read through, think about how each engine could show up both in your own practice and in theirs.

THE SIX EVIDENCE ENGINES

Each Evidence Engine is a system that creates, captures, and communicates proof. Together, they feed every part of a brand's reputation: integrity, competence, community, and narrative. When all six are running, your client's brand stops chasing attention and starts creating a gravitational pull. People come to them naturally because they believe what they see.

EVIDENCE ENGINES

DELIVERY ENGINE PROVES COMPETENCE	**COMMUNITY ENGINE** PROVES COMMUNITY	**TRANSPARENCY ENGINE** PROVES INTEGRITY
EDUCATION ENGINE PROVES COMPETENCE + NARRATIVE	**RECOGNITION ENGINE** PROVES EXTERNAL CREDIBILITY	**REFLECTION ENGINE** PROVES INTEGRITY

1 Delivery Engines: Prove Competence

Delivery Engines are the most direct trust builders. They show that your client can deliver what they promise, reliably and consistently. Their purpose is to prove that the craft works in the real world.

Examples include:
- Case studies, project breakdowns, and testimonials
- Before-and-after visuals or process stories
- Honest reflections on what worked and what didn't
- Progress updates or project milestones

Every time a promise is kept, that's living proof of competence. These engines show that the work isn't just theory. It performs under pressure.

2 Community Engines: Prove Community

Community Engines are social proof in motion. They show that your client isn't working in isolation, that others believe in what they're doing and want to be part of it.

Examples include:
- Client shout-outs and joint projects
- Collaborations or partnerships
- Celebrating shared wins
- Testimonials and referrals

A brand without community is an island. Community Engines turn followers into fans and fans into advocates who help carry your client's reputation further than they could alone.

3 Transparency Engines: Prove Integrity

Transparency Engines show the how behind the what. They make the process visible. This isn't vulnerability for attention; it's about how honesty builds credibility.

Examples include:
- Sharing why certain design choices were made
- Talking openly about pricing or lessons learned
- Showing behind-the-scenes reality rather than perfection

Transparency removes the mystery that creates mistrust. It shows that your client doesn't just believe in their work, but also in the values behind it.

4 Education Engines: Prove Competence and Narrative

Teaching is one of the purest forms of evidence. When your client can simplify their craft and share it with others, it shows mastery and generosity.

Examples include:
- Process explainers or bite-sized tutorials
- Frameworks, principles, or creative lessons
- Real-world takeaways from experience

Every time they teach, they show confidence and care. These engines tell the story of competence in real time. It says, "I know what I'm doing, and I want to help you, too."

5 Recognition Engines: Prove External Credibility

Recognition Engines are all about third-party validation. They prove that others see and appreciate the quality of the work.

Examples include:
- Awards, features, guest talks, or press mentions
- Client testimonials or shoutouts from other reputable humans
- Certifications, accreditations, or trusted collaborations

Recognition Engines amplify the evidence through others. They show that the proof holds up outside your client's own circle.

6 Reflection Engines: Prove Integrity

Reflection Engines are where the human part of the brand comes through. They show not just what your client does but who they're becoming.

Examples include:
- Annual reflections or "what I learned" posts
- Personal growth moments or stories about challenges
- Thoughts on values, mindset, or creative purpose

Reflection Engines give credibility a heartbeat. They show depth and remind people that there's a real person behind the proof. That's where long-term trust begins.

Each engine fuels a different part of the brand's reputation. Delivery builds competence. Transparency builds integrity. Community and Recognition create belonging. Education and Reflection give the brand a story that connects everything together.

When all of these work in unison, a brand becomes believable, relatable, and magnetic. It feels trustworthy because every signal points to something real. The right people begin to gather around it, not because they were targeted, but because they felt something genuine.

This is the real magic of credibility strategy. Instead of trying to reach everyone, your client builds the kind of brand that quietly reaches the right ones. The evidence economy is calm and doesn't need to shout. It's built on consistent behaviour, not random buzz. When your clients work this way, they stop trying to impress strangers and start connecting with believers. The wrong people drift away, and the right people stay. That's exactly how it should be.

Once your clients start using these engines, they realise something interesting. They're not creating marketing anymore. They're documenting proof. And that's a huge shift.

Technically, they are still creating content, because everything they share lives out in the world. But this is a different kind of content. It's not made for algorithms or attention. It's made for trust. Every post, project, or story becomes another piece of evidence that compounds over time, not to entertain people but to reassure them that what your client does is real.

Over time, that memory becomes recognition. And recognition is what transforms a small brand into a known and trusted one. Proof builds belief. Belief builds belonging. Belonging builds reputation. You know the score by now.

Help your clients see that. Help them shift from content to credibility, from attention to evidence, from trying to be seen to proving they're worth seeing. The right people don't come from being everywhere all the time. They come from trust. And good reputations, as you already know, are always built on trust.

THE TRUTH IS, THE BRANDS THAT WIN AREN'T THE LOUDEST. THEY'RE THE ONES THAT BACK UP WHAT THEY SAY WITH PROOF.

Chapter Thirty –

LEAD GENERATION WITHOUT OVERWHELM

Right—you know how to attract the right people through credibility and proof. Now, it's time to keep those humans close without losing your head in the process. This is where a lot of brands get it wrong, and I'll hold my hand up because for a long time I was terrible at follow-up. The second someone showed interest, the panic would creep in. Suddenly it was "We need a funnel," "We need a content plan," "We need to automate everything." And before long, the human side of the brand disappeared.

The truth is that lead generation doesn't need to feel like a job in itself. It's not a separate part of the work and it definitely doesn't need to be a flat-out sprint. It's simply about staying connected with people who already believe in you. It's about building relationships, not collecting names, and doing it in a way that feels aligned to you personally.

When you strip it back, a lead is just someone who's curious. Someone who's halfway convinced that your client might be the right fit but needs a bit more proof before they're ready to take the next step. The mistake most people make is trying to force that belief instead of earning it. They start pestering too early and it pushes people away.

That's what this chapter is about. Helping your clients build trust through care. It's about looking after the people who are already looking at them. And honestly, it's about helping you do the same. Because the more you treat leads like people, the easier it becomes to build genuine, lasting connections that keep everyone happy.

Good lead generation is just good relationship building. It's following up with people because you care, not because you need something. It's remembering names when possible, sending thank-yous, sharing something useful, or checking in a few months later with a genuine "How's it going?" Those little things stack up in the old trust and credibility bank.

When you work like this, you stop seeing marketing as a series of tasks and start seeing it as a rhythm. A quiet, consistent flow that keeps you connected to the people who matter. It can be embedded into any business system or process. You just need a few good habits that keep the conversation alive.

Here are a few simple things that can make a huge difference, both for you and your clients:

- **Reach out to one past client each week to see how they're doing.**
- **Share one small story that shows what you've been working on or learning lately.**
- **Reply properly to a comment, message, or email with curiosity.**
- **Ask a happy client for a referral.**
- **Thank someone publicly for their support or collaboration.**

These small actions compound over time. They keep you visible to the right people without burning you out and they continuously remind people that you care. They build trust slowly and naturally. And I get it, the slow game doesn't sound that exciting. Everyone wants quick wins and big leaps because that's what the internet tells us happens. But the reality is, this is the kind of work that quietly builds momentum. If you want to build a life that's yours, and help your clients build one that's theirs, this is the path. The effort you put in now will make everything easier later. You won't have to chase every new trend or sprint after every shiny idea just to stay relevant. You'll already be building something steady and sustainable—a reputation that grows at its own pace and lasts.

And for your clients, the same idea applies. The goal isn't to impress people with noise, it's to connect through carefully thought-out interactions. When they check in with customers after a purchase, ask for honest feedback, or share small behind-the-scenes moments, they show they value people, not just their transactions. Those actions build emotional memory. People might forget a product they bought, but they'll never forget how a brand made them feel.

The real secret to sustainable lead generation is this: connection over conversion.

If your client can master that mindset, everything else gets easier. They won't need to shout, they won't need to hustle—they'll simply need to show up, stay curious, and be a good human.

Your role in all this is to help them build the kind of systems that make care sustainable. And I know you might not see this as your job right now, but this is exactly where designers can become truly indispensable. When you start helping your clients build small keep-in-touch systems, when you help them come up with ways to stay connected and care for their people, you move beyond being the person who just makes things look good. You become a creative partner. Someone who thinks about their reputation. Someone who adds real, ongoing value.

That's a power move. It's what separates a service provider from a trusted ally. The kind of ally clients come back to again and again because you didn't just help them launch, you helped them grow.

And the same goes for you. You don't need to fill your calendar to build a thriving design business. You just need to look after the people who already believe in what you do. The best clients often come from the smallest gestures, the kind follow-up, the check-in, the shared lesson. The designers who stay booked aren't necessarily the ones with the biggest reach. They're the ones who build the strongest relationships . . . and it's much easier to keep a client than it is to find a new one.

If you take care of the people who already believe in what you do, they'll take care of the rest. They become advocates and they become the community that keeps your brand alive long after the project is done. Lead generation without overwhelm isn't about doing less. It's about doing what matters most. It's about being generous with your attention.

Next, we'll look at how to learn from these connections, validate what's working, improve what isn't working, and keep building momentum with confidence. Because once you've built relationships that feel real, you've got everything you need to grow without the panic.

LINCOLN
DESIGN
Company
Canva

DESIGN
ØR DIE

Chapter Thirty-One –

VALIDATE EARLY, LEARN FAST

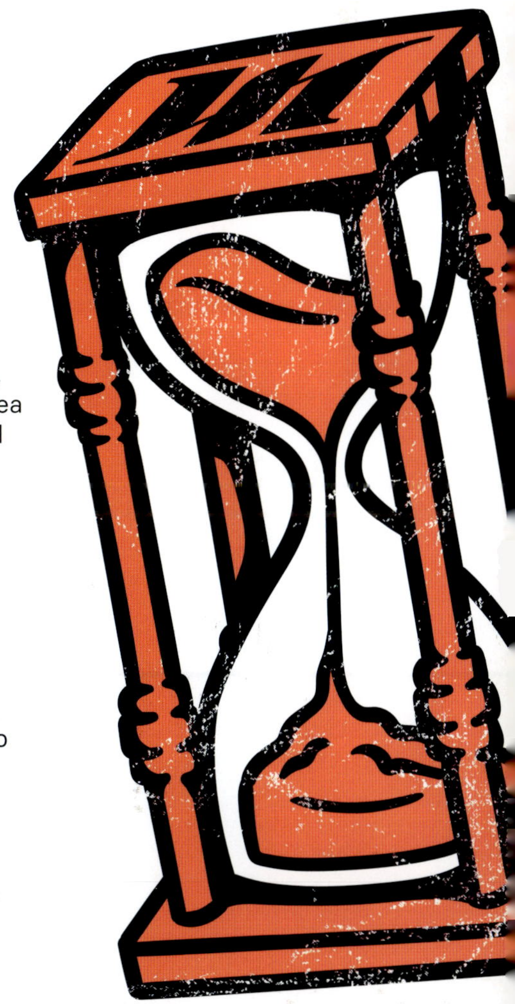

Everything you've read in this book so far is, in its own way, my collection of evidence. Every framework, story, and process has been shaped by years of trying, testing, asking for feedback, and learning from both the wins and the wibbly wobblies. Nothing here was plucked out of thin air. It has all been refined and validated through real work with real people.

Over the last twenty years, I've gathered this evidence like an accountant gathers receipts. From coaching calls, brand workshops, messy projects, design meltdowns, and the late-night reflections that only come after a job goes sideways. The Five Idea Keys, the MVB mindset, even this very book—none of it appeared fully formed. It all started as an idea that was tested, stretched, and simplified until it worked.

That's exactly what validation is. It's not about being right straight away. It's about learning what's real. It's about collecting your own evidence through practice and proof, because whether you're shaping a brand, designing a new offer, or trying to find your next client, you never really know if something works until it meets the world.

This is the stage where we help our clients learn in public. We help them turn guesswork into guidance. We want to encourage them to test early and learn fast so they stop waiting for perfection and start trusting the process.

Validation is not about seeking approval. It's about collecting evidence.

The goal is not to please everyone. It's to understand how the right people respond.

Too many clients launch their ideas and sit back waiting for the world to applaud them from the rooftops. They assume silence means failure and criticism means rejection, but in reality, both are data, and data is good. We need to get our clients to pay attention to what lands, what confuses, and what makes people smile or scroll quickly past.

As designers, we can turn raw reactions into usable insights. When a stranger comments, "I love this but I don't quite get what you do," that's not an insult. That's a gift. It means something in the message or visuals needs tightening. When someone says, "This feels exactly like me," that's evidence that the tone and design are aligned. Both responses are useful.

That's the beauty of validation. Once your clients see it as learning rather than losing, everything changes. They stop taking feedback personally and they start taking it seriously. We can help them build systems for gathering and filtering feedback in a way that keeps them moving forward.

Start super small. Encourage them to test their ideas with people. They don't need to open the floodgates and invite the whole internet in. They can start with a small group of trusted customers or community members.

Ask a few simple questions like:

- **What caught your attention first?**
- **What confused you?**
- **What made you want to know more?**

Those three questions can tell you more about a brand's clarity than a thousand likes ever could. Once that feedback comes in, teach your clients to filter it, because not all feedback is created equal. Some comes from love, some from ego, some from fear. The trick is to spot the difference. Or, as I once heard when I was a young lad, "Opinions are like arseholes . . . everyone's got one, and most of them stink." Real validation comes from people who fit the brand's audience, not from random opinions online.

One simple way to filter is to link everything back to the work you did earlier in the process. Revisit the Five Idea Keys. Does the feedback align with the truth of the brand? Does it reflect what the brand set out to communicate? If it does, pay attention. If it doesn't, let it go.

This approach turns testing into an ongoing practice rather than a stressful event. It keeps your clients curious and engaged without letting blind panic take over. They don't have to wait six months for results or reinvent everything when one comment throws them off. They can make small, meaningful adjustments as they go.

It's easy to think validation ends once something works, but the truth is that it never stops. Brands continuously evolve. Audiences continuously shift. What felt perfect last year might need a total refresh today. The goal isn't to build something that never changes. It's to build something that can keep iterating. That's why I love the MVB.

And that's what you're really doing when you help your clients validate early and learn fast. You're teaching them how to stay flexible. The most successful brands don't fear feedback. They feed on it. They invite it in, process it and use it to make smarter decisions.

So, when you're guiding your clients through this stage, remind them that validation isn't about their worth and it's not about winning approval. It's about gathering proof.

Proof that the message is clear.
Proof that the visuals connect.
Proof that the brand feels right.

When they have that, they have direction. And direction builds confidence. The faster you learn, the faster you grow, and the clearer it all feels. That's what this chapter is really about: building that juicy evidence. Because evidence is what turns ideas into brands, and brands into reputations that last.

LEARN FAST

earning from Dan Janssen at Into The Woods 2023

Chapter Thirty-Two –

SHOW UP CONSISTENTLY

I love going to the beach with my wife and my son, Rocco. It's my wife's favourite place in the world. She always says the sea has its own rhythm. She can sit there for hours just watching it move. The waves come in, the waves go out. The pattern never really changes, yet it's never exactly the same either. You can trust it. You don't stand there wondering if the next wave will arrive . . . you know it will. There's something calming about that. It's predictable, but alive.

I used to think rhythm like that only existed in nature, but the longer I've been building brands, the more I've realised that the best ones move the same way. They've got their own pulse. They breathe. They build trust through patterns that feel natural and predictable. They don't need to scream for attention or constantly reinvent themselves. People come back because they know what to expect.

> **THAT QUIET CONSISTENCY BUILDS COMFORT AND CONFIDENCE, AND THOSE TWO THINGS ARE LIKE GOLD DUST IN A NOISY WORLD.**

That's really what we want to help our clients build. A rhythm that people can rely on. Something that feels steady, human, and familiar. Because humans are pattern-spotting machines. Our brains are constantly scanning the world asking, "Can I predict what happens next?" When we can, we relax. When we can't, the brain starts doing that weird little panic shuffle.

That's the amygdala doing its ancient job. That pair of tiny almond-shaped lumps tucked deep in your head is quietly running the show. That's the alarm bell that's kept humans alive for a few hundred thousand years. When things feel steady and familiar, it chills out and lets you enjoy your cup of tea. But when things get unpredictable, it goes full foghorn mode. That's why people freak out when their favourite brand suddenly changes everything overnight. The chaos doesn't just confuse their brains; it makes their whole nervous system twitch.

That's why consistency matters. It helps people feel safe. It tells them that what they saw yesterday still matters today. And that's really what trust is . . . people feeling safe with you. Predictability calms the mind and opens the door to belief.

Our job as designers is to help our clients build that kind of stability. Not just in how their brand looks, but in how it behaves. It's about helping them find a rhythm that suits them—a pace they can actually live with. Some brands move fast, others slow. Some bounce around with crazy energy, others take their time. There's no single tempo that works for everyone, but there's always one that feels right.

We can help them find it. Ask questions like, "What pace feels natural to you?" or "How often can you show up without it feeling like a chore?" Because when a rhythm feels forced, it snaps. But when it feels natural, it flows. That's when consistency stops being a job and starts being part of who they are.

Rhythm is powerful because it gives people something steady to hold onto while still leaving space for the little blips that make life interesting. The waves never crash in exactly the same way, but they always come back. That's what makes them comforting. Predictability keeps things calm; flexibility keeps things alive. Too much chaos and people lose trust. Too much sameness and they lose interest. But when you find that sweet middle bit, the whole thing starts to breathe. That's the kind of rhythm that builds long-term trust.

Consistency isn't about repetition for the sake of it. It's not about posting every day or shouting the same message over and over again. It's about showing up with the same truth, the same energy, and the same care. Every small, predictable action builds familiarity. Every familiar moment builds trust. And trust, as we already know, is the foundation of reputation.

As designers, we can help our clients build systems that make that consistency possible. Not robotic routines, but human rhythms. We can help them plan how they show up, how they talk, how they deliver, and how they follow up. Every touchpoint should feel like part of the same beat. When that rhythm settles in, the brand starts to feel alive. Not rushed. Not random. Just steady and strong.

And it helps us, too. The more we understand our clients' rhythm, the better we can design for it. We can build systems that actually work in their world, not just in a shiny presentation deck. We can help them create something sustainable, a brand that moves at a pace they can genuinely keep up with. That's how we move from decorators to true creative partners, the kind of people clients trust to keep things steady when the waves get choppy.

Over time, that rhythm starts to compound. Every consistent action builds a little more belief. It reassures people that what they see today is what they'll see tomorrow. It quietly says, "You're in good hands." And that's exactly what trust feels like.

If the beach has taught me anything, it's that rhythm doesn't need to be forced. The waves don't rush, they don't panic, but they never stop either. That's the rhythm I want us to help our clients find. One that's natural, human, and real. Because when people can trust the rhythm of a brand, they start to move with it. They start to believe in it. And that's how good reputations are built.

Conclusion –

THE REAL BRAND LIFE

I hope by now that this book has done its job. Not in the sense of giving you another checklist for branding, but in helping you see the whole thing a little differently. You're not just someone who makes things for other people. You're someone building a reputation of your own. You've now got the tools to do it with intention, and you know how to shape ideas properly, how to move them into the world without panic, and how to build something that lasts. More importantly, you've seen that you have far more control than you've been led to believe.

The creative world has a funny way of making you forget who's actually in control. Before long, you start believing that control belongs to other people, that you're supposed to follow their rules and play their game. But you're not. You've had the steering wheel the whole time. You've always had the power to decide what you stand for and how you show up. That's really what this book was written for—to give you a better way of seeing things, to put you back in charge of your own creativity, your reputation, and the way you build your life around them.

Branding isn't something that belongs to businesses or agencies with big budgets. It belongs to people, too, because at its heart, it's simply the act of making meaning visible. When you start to see it that way, everything shifts. You stop building for performance and start building for proof. You stop chasing recognition and focus on earning a reputation. And over time, you begin to live what I call The Real Brand Life, that place where your creativity, your character, and your career move together in the same steady rhythm.

You've already learned what rhythm means in your work. Now, it's time to live it. That rhythm isn't about balance or control. It's about movement. It changes shape depending on the season you're in. You can feel it when it clicks, when the work flows, when the energy feels right, when what you're making actually feels like you. Your rhythm might look messy to someone else, but if it keeps you creating, keep it. The world doesn't need more perfectly scheduled creatives. It needs more people brave enough to listen to their own weird tempo.

That rhythm will change, and that's completely fine. It'll shift from year to year, project to project, sometimes even day to day, depending on whether life's playing nice or throwing curveballs. There'll be seasons where you're charging ahead full of energy and ideas, and others where you're crawling through mud, wondering if you've lost it completely. Both count; both matter. They're part of the job description. The trick is to stay awake through it all and pay attention to what kind of work you're actually doing and why you're doing it, because that's what keeps you grounded.

> **"THE WORLD DOESN'T NEED MORE PERFECTLY SCHEDULED CREATIVES. IT NEEDS MORE PEOPLE BRAVE ENOUGH TO LISTEN TO THEIR OWN WEIRD TEMPO."**

The REAL BRAND LIFE!

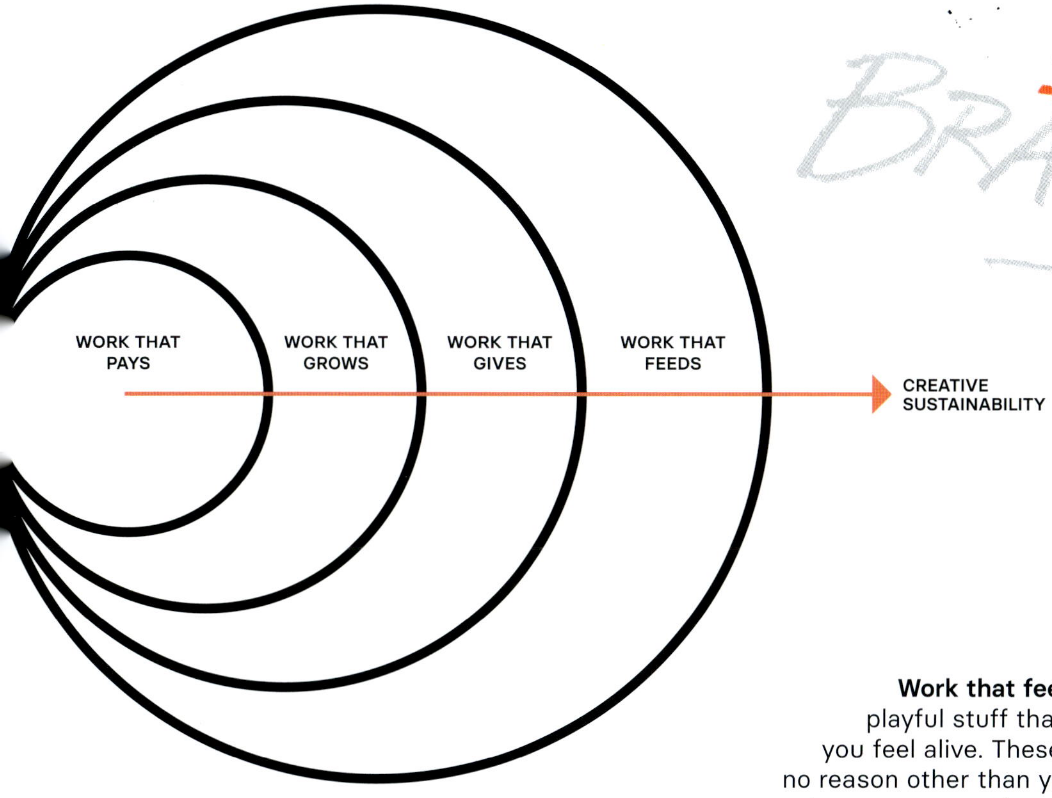

Over the years, I've realised that to stay sane and still love what I do, I've had to break my work down into four simple types. It wasn't some grand plan or clever system at first, just a bit of self-preservation that actually worked.

There are four types of work that keep things in check.

Work that pays is the foundation. It's the steady, dependable work that keeps life moving and the bills handled. These are the projects that fund your freedom and give you the stability to make better choices. Without this, nothing else happens.

Work that grows is the stretch. It's the work that challenges you, teaches you something new, or pushes you into unfamiliar territory. It might be uncomfortable, but it's how you level up and stop yourself from going stale.

Work that gives is the connection. It's how you share what you've learned: the mentoring, the helping, the small moments of generosity that remind you creativity's not a solo sport. This kind of work builds trust and reputation because people remember how you made them feel.

Work that feeds is the refill. It's the personal, playful stuff that exists purely because it makes you feel alive. These are the things you make for no reason other than you enjoy making them. They recharge your creative energy and keep everything else running with heart.

You don't need to balance these perfectly—just notice which one you've been ignoring. If you've been buried in work that pays, feed yourself. If you're too comfortable, grow. If you've been isolated, give. Awareness is what keeps your creativity sustainable and allows you to bring more intention into your days.

When you work like this, your reputation builds naturally. You don't need to shout about who you are, because it will show up in how you work, how you treat people, and what you share. Integrity, competence, community, and narrative are not theory—they're the quiet habits that create trust. When those four move together, you build something unshakable, a brand that doesn't depend on hype but on history, a reputation that grows from truth and real receipts.

The creative world we live in isn't a sprint; it's a long, strange, beautiful marathon. There are stretches where nothing seems to happen and others where everything lands at once. Some projects fall flat, some clients disappear, and some weeks, you'll question whether you've still got it. You haven't lost it; you're just between rhythms. Every creative goes through that. The ones who last are the ones who keep showing up, stay curious, and understand that the quiet patches aren't failures, they're just part of the process.

The Real Brand Life isn't about endless growth, it's about continuity. It's about staying in love with your craft long enough that it becomes part of who you are. The longer you stay in rhythm, the more your reputation compounds. You stop chasing the next big thing because you realise the real work is already happening in every act of consistency, every decision made with integrity, every project that carries a bit of your heart. That's where the brand lives—not in your logo, but in your evidence.

Now that you've got the tools, you don't need permission to begin. You don't need a bigger following, a better website, or a grand plan. You just need to start showing your proof one idea, one client, one conversation at a time. You don't have to be the loudest, you just have to be the truest version of you. The world needs more people like you, people who are willing to be real, who care about building something genuine instead of tearing others down just to look clever on Instagram. We've got enough critics, commentators, and keyboard experts. What we need are more doers. People who create, share, and show up with honesty.

> **I WANT YOU TO BUILD A CREATIVE LIFE THAT ACTUALLY FEELS LIKE YOURS. TO WAKE UP EXCITED BY WHAT YOU'RE WORKING ON, NOT DRAINED BY WHO YOU'RE PRETENDING TO BE.**

To be known not for your hustle, but for your honesty. That's what happens when you align your creativity, your character, and your career. That's when the brand stops being something you do and starts being something you live.

Once you reach that point, my friend, the pressure starts to lift. You don't need to perform or prove that you belong. You just get to create freely, openly, messily, and magically. That's the real reward. It's not about recognition or success; it's about the peace that comes from doing it your way. Remember, you are more than your job. You're not just a pair of hands for hire. You are a role the world needs, the creative partner who brings ideas to life, one proof-filled decision at a time.

So, as you get close to closing this book, I hope you feel that quiet sense of relief that reminds you that you can absolutely do this. You already have everything you need: the thinking, the tools, the talent, and the truth. The rest is time and rhythm. Go and make the work that proves what you're capable of. Go and live your version of The Real Brand Life, whatever that looks like for you. And most of all, enjoy it, because you've worked hard for this and you deserve every bit of what comes next. And hey, if you ever want to join a bunch of super-duper people who are building The Real Brand Life, too, you know where to find me.

Stay sassy.

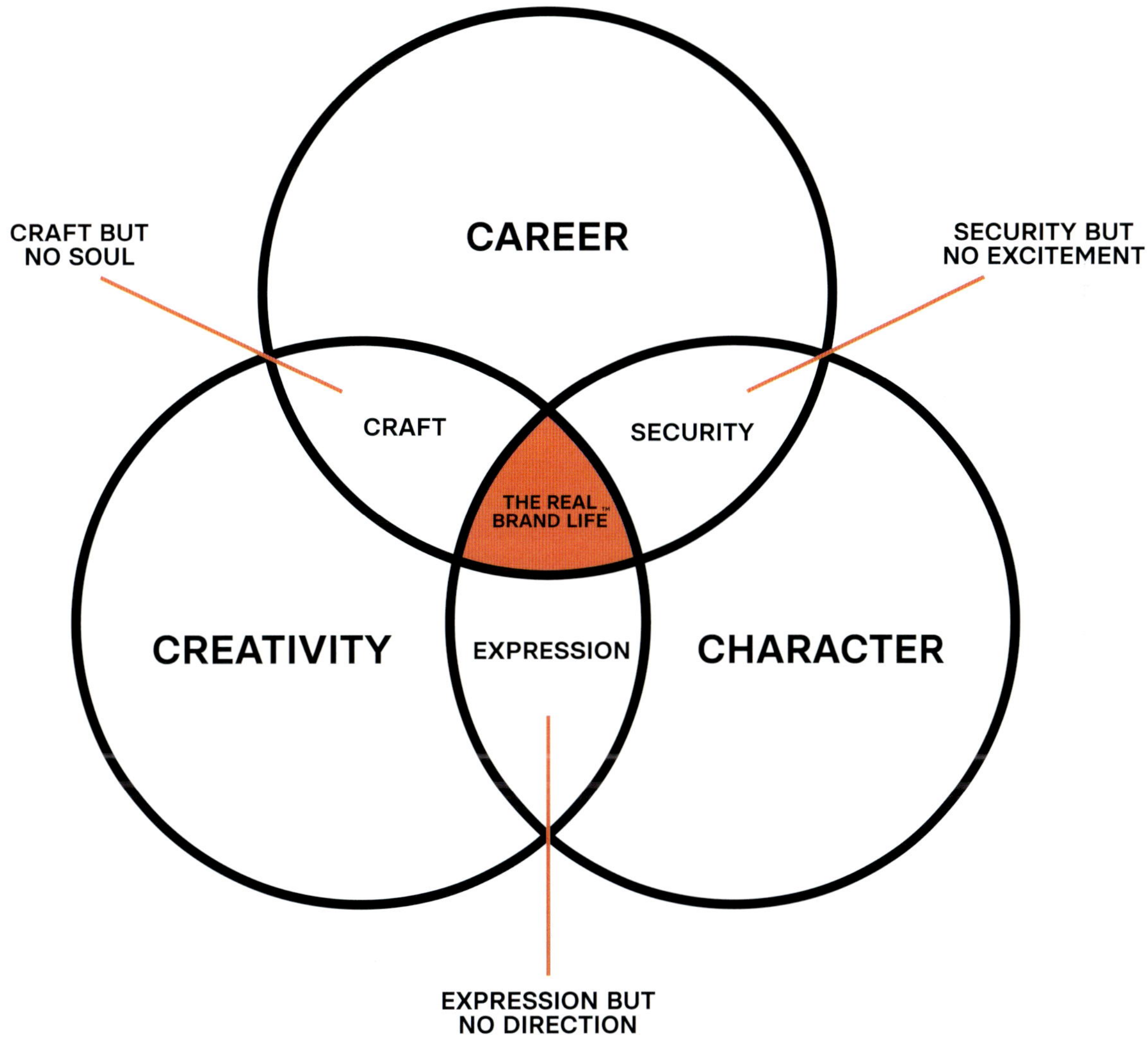
CAREER
CREATIVITY
CHARACTER
CRAFT
SECURITY
EXPRESSION
THE REAL BRAND LIFE™
CRAFT BUT NO SOUL
SECURITY BUT NO EXCITEMENT
EXPRESSION BUT NO DIRECTION

A LETTER FROM DEBBIE MILLMAN

Debbie Millman is a designer, author, educator, curator, and host of the pioneering podcast *Design Matters*.

Named one of Fast Company's Most Creative People, one of the Most Influential Graphic Designer[s] working today by Graphic Design USA, and a SUCCESS Magazine Woman of Influence, by *Success* magazine, Debbie Millman has built a remarkable career at the intersection of design, storytelling, and cultural commentary.

Dear James,

This is what I believe about the work we do:

I think that brands make the biggest impact when they help people imagine what doesn't yet exist. Brands today can't rely on logos, taglines, or perfectly polished campaigns. They need to stand for something, to lead with purpose and values, and to be transparent about who they are and how they operate. That means taking some risks. Brands must represent a point of view so people know what they are buying into—and as importantly—what they won't.

People deserve honesty over perfection in their allegiances to products and things, and brands need to be communicating with a voice that tells the truth. It is our responsibility to avoid corporate marketing bingo and mission statements that read as word salads. The real work of branding now shows up in how people actually experience them: the way a product is made, the way a message is shared, the way a company behaves day-to-day. The experience needs to be more personal and meaningful, while also respecting privacy and being honest about data. It has to be sustainable, not as a marketing veneer but as a genuine commitment to doing less harm. And because culture moves so quickly, brands need to embrace speed and experimentation, showing up in ways that feel alive rather than scripted. Most of all, they have to shift from broadcasting at people to building with them.

The future of branding is being shaped by a deeper need for meaning. People are tired of noise and empty promises; they deserve veracity, humanity, and a sense of belonging. Brands will need to reflect the complexity of our identities, show a real commitment to sustainability, and move at the speed of culture without losing their integrity.

Technology and AI are accelerating the pace, but what people will remember are the stories, the communities, and the values that are real and measurable. And for those of us that are afraid of AI taking our jobs and livelihood, I witnessed the same discussion about what computers would do to our business 40 years ago. And yes, some jobs were lost in our community, but hundreds of thousands of job were created for designers via the very devices we design everything we make now.

More than ever, brands can't just sell—they'll need to stand for something, invite people in, and create experiences that make life feel richer, more connected, and more hopeful. As the people that steer, lead, create, and participate in the business of design and branding, we must courageously lead a path to new frontiers.

Let's do this.
Debbie

Conclusion –

ACKNOWLEDGMENTS

I could write a whole other book trying to acknowledge everyone who has positively influenced me over my lifetime. But during the writing of this book, there are a few people I really want to shout out.

Kate Martin, a.k.a. wifey:
You've stuck with me through thick and thin. You always pick me up when I'm down, and you're always there to listen to both my good days and my bad. You are my best friend and the love of my life. Thank you for your constant encouragement, even when you think my ideas are a little silly.

Rocco Martin, a.k.a. my son:
You don't yet know how much you've inspired me since arriving on this planet, but the last three years with you have meant everything to me. Watching you grow, play, and smile has been a complete joy. I'll always sing "Hakuna Matata" with you, and I'll never stop trying my hardest to be the best dad I can be for you.

Tyler Tolson, a.k.a. Tenacious T:
Thank you for believing in me. Thank you for everything you've taught me about life and running a creative business. And most of all, thank you for the sparkly drinks we often enjoy while driving around Cache Valley, Utah. Here's to the future, sir.

Dan Janssen, a.k.a. boss man:
It's an honor to be part of the Lincoln Design crew. Thank you for making one of my dreams come true. I'll always represent LDC in the best way I can. Thank you for your support, belief, and friendship over the years—it truly means the world to me.

Kevin Finn, a.k.a. Finny:
Thank you for always replying to my texts, weird questions, and brand-world rants. Having you in my world has made a huge positive difference in every aspect of my life. I've learned so much from you, and I'll always be thankful for the role you've played in this book. Your wisdom and knowledge have been a huge asset.

Kiel Tillman and Paul Balfe a.k.a. Pennybridge:
It's been an honour to work on this book with you. Thank you for your energy, super slick skills, and care. This book looks as good as it does because you were both involved. I hope you've enjoyed this journey as much as I have. You both are freaking rad.

Kate Martin

Rocco Martin

Tyler Tolson

Dan Janssen

Kevin Finn

Paul Balfe

Kiel Tillman

Conclusion –

ABOUT THE AUTHOR

James Martin, known online as Made by James, has spent the last two decades building brands, communities, and ideas—not just for clients but also for himself. He sees his role less as a designer and more as a liberator of ideas. Whether for a founder with a half-formed concept or one of his own restless sparks, his obsession is taking something raw and turning it into something real.

That curiosity has led him to partnerships and advisory roles with some of the biggest names in design, including Affinity, Canva, and Lincoln Design Co. Alongside that, he's built his own ventures: a design studio, bestselling books, courses, communities, SaaS tools, live events, and stages where he shares what he's learned. Each project is another experiment in proving that ideas matter most when they're given the chance to breathe.

James doesn't buy into complexity for the sake of it. Design and branding should empower, not gatekeep. His contrarian streak pushes him to strip away jargon, challenge the defaults, and make the creative world more accessible for everyone.

At the core of everything he builds is a philosophy he calls The Real Brand Life, his own take on *ikigai.* It's the space where creativity, character, and career overlap. The place where what you make, who you are, and how you live finally align. That's what he teaches through his books, frameworks, and communities: to help other creatives and founders find that same rhythm, build brands without panic, and actually enjoy the process.

Today, through his frameworks like the Five Idea Keys, the Reputation Grid, and his love for the Minimum Viable Brand (MVB), James continues to help people turn ideas into proof and proof into reputation.

He lives on the South Coast of the UK with his wife, Kate, their son, Rocco, and an ever-growing collection of sketchbooks, framed art, and tattoo ideas.

LINCOLN
SEEK & DESTROY

INDEX

SOUND
BEHAVE
LOOK
REAL